OPERATIONS
Due Diligence

An M&A Guide for Investors and Business

JAMES F. GREBEY

New York Chicago San Francisco Lisbon London Madrid Mexico City
Milan New Delhi San Juan Seoul Singapore Sydney Toronto

ISBN 978-0-07-177761-2
MHID 0-07-177761-X

e-ISBN 978-0-07-177851-0
e-MHID 0-07-177851-9

This publication is designed to provide accurate and authoritative information in regard to the subject matter covered. It is sold with the understanding that neither the author nor the publisher is engaged in rendering legal, accounting, securities trading, or other professional services. If legal advice or other expert assistance is required, the services of a competent professional person should be sought.

—From a Declaration of Principles Jointly Adopted by a Committee of the American Bar Association and a Committee of Publishers and Associations

McGraw-Hill books are available at special quantity discounts to use as premiums and sales promotions or for use in corporate training programs. To contact a representative, please e-mail us at bulksales@mcgraw-hill.com.

This book is printed on acid-free paper.

To Winnie . . . above everything else

CONTENTS

PART TWO

EXPLORING IN DEPTH   41

Chapter 7

Chapter 8

Chapter 9

PREFACE

Operations Due Diligence has emerged from my personal experiences while working with a wide range of businesses owners, managers, and investors. It represents two sides of the same coin. It was written as a due diligence guide for investors trying to determine the sustainability of a business, and it also serves as a much needed operations checklist for managers and business owners trying to improve the sustainability of their business. It is the result of many hard lessons learned while trying to help these groups grow their businesses.

I don't feel that my experiences have been unique. My work has been "in the trenches," tugging, pulling, trying to make things happen. Some things have worked, and, I must admit, some have not. In some cases, the lesson has been in the form of a mental note: Don't ever do that again. There are lots of people working in those same trenches every day. They include investors who are trying to figure out how to capture their next opportunity while minimizing their risk and business owners and managers who are struggling to improve their business.

Operations Due Diligence isn't an academic dissertation. It is a very practical look at what makes businesses operate successfully and a "roll up your sleeves and get to work" approach that will be a useful tool that I hope will help the people in the trenches.

In 1971, I worked in a shipyard in Pascagoula, Mississippi. At that time chess was a resurging fad. During lunch breaks the chess boards would be pulled out and the games would begin. Everyone was either playing chess or trying to get a chance to play a guy named Phil. Phil had a reputation for being the best chess player in our group. Everyone wanted to be able to claim that he or she had beaten Phil. Phil was not a chess master, and he was beaten on occasion. He just seemed to win . . . a lot. Phil was very willing to share what he knew about the game with everyone. He hadn't memorized all of the fancy openings and moves, although he had many that experience had taught him. He had created a list of 10 basic, very practical, rules. Rules like "Always move your rook to an open column" and "Always take an even trade."

I still have a copy of Phil's rules, and I still use them today.

My intent with *Operations Due Diligence* was to provide a set of very pragmatic rules that would help investors and businesses win more than they lose.

One lesson we have recently learned is that any business can fail. Enron proved that large businesses can fail as spectacularly as small businesses can. Determining how sustainable a business will be requires a deep analysis and exploration of its operations. Businesses must constantly challenge themselves to improve their operations. They have to take the time to analyze and mitigate their risks, and they must constantly seek to capture opportunities to advance in order to improve their chances for success. Investors use the due diligence process to assess the operational risks and opportunities that a business presents for them.

Assessing the operations of a business is a difficult task, but it is key to understanding its sustainability. How do investors effectively assess a business's operations during their due diligence?

While writing *Operations Due Diligence*, one of the problems I had to solve was the organization and presentation of the material effectively in a single volume. The result is a pragmatic series of questions, presented with examples that place them in historical and practical context around nine assessment areas. These areas serve to highlight and focus the Operations Due Diligence activities.

In his book *Built to Last* (HarperCollins, 1994), Jim Collins described how important it is for a business to develop its sustaining infrastructure. And in his second book *Good to Great* (HarperCollins, 2001), Collins described how to grow a business into a great business. Collins's works have become a cornerstone for building sustainable businesses. Assuming that a business has followed that advice, the question remains: How can investors assess how well the business has succeeded in implementing its operations infrastructure?

Operations Due Diligence answers that question.

Finally, throughout *Operations Due Diligence*, I relied on historical references and relevant stories as examples that will provide a context for the questions I present. I did this both to help readers understand the concepts and to make reading the book more enjoyable. I hope you enjoy it. I encourage readers to share their own stories with me.

You can e-mail me at jim@grebey.com.

ACKNOWLEDGMENTS

I would like to acknowledge the following people for their role in making this book a reality:

Winnie, James, Jesse, Sean, Dan, Denise, Dale, Tanner, Chase, Aaron, Myah, Bud, Carol, and Marie for their constant love and encouragement

My agent, Lynne Rabinoff, for taking a chance on a new author and leading the way

Mike, Diane, Dave, Thom, Nancy, Terry, Bud, Hap, Henry, and Paul for being my sounding boards and honest agents

Jennifer Ashkenazy, Jane Palmieri, and the professional staff at McGraw-Hill who brought this all together

Thank you for all of your help.

PART ONE

Planning Your Assessment

Due diligence: To gain what is owed through care and perseverance.

—*Webster's Dictionary*

CHAPTER 1

Due Diligence

"We are striking it big in the electric light, better than my vivid imagination first conceived. Where this thing is going to stop Lord only knows."

—Thomas Edison, Edison Museum, Fort Myers, Florida, October 1879

During the mid-nineteenth century, the homes and businesses in most large cities relied on gas lamps for light. Natural gas piped into the home was considered the modern alternative to the oil lamps and candles people had previously used. Vast networks of underground pipes supplied the gas, and the utility companies grew large by expanding their pipelines to consumers who had few alternatives. The network of gas pipelines grew out from the cities to reach more customers, and as the pipelines grew, the distribution and maintenance of the pipelines became an enormous and expensive burden.

Thomas Edison had the vision to recognize that the electric light could become the alternative to gas lamps. He began his mission to generate electric power that would be cheaper to produce and would provide a new, cleaner source of illumination. To that end, Edison formed the Edison Electric Light Company in 1878 with a group of investors including J. P. Morgan and the Vanderbilts, who advanced him $30,000 for research and development.

The Edison Electric Light Company eventually became known as General Electric. In many ways, Edison's search continues today with the need for visionaries who recognize the potential of renewable sources of energy like solar power, which is a cleaner and more efficient alternative to gas- or coal-generated power.

Investing in a business today is, and always has been, a risky venture. When Thomas Edison sought investors for Edison Electric Light Company, he had to first convince his investors that this new product, the electric light, would someday replace the oil and natural gas lamps they were already using. The investors had to take a risk and be willing to share

Edison's vision of a future, yet unknown industry. They had to be sold on this vision of the new technology sufficiently to invest their money when others were not able to envision a city strung out with electric utility poles. He had to sell the investors on what would become a truly disruptive technology.

The history of investing is a history of risks taken and opportunities seized. Investors are willing to take these chances because this is the well-established path to potential large returns on their money.

While some investors have captured opportunities and realized these returns, there are many others who have made the wrong choice and lost. Some investors have succeeded against what seemed like terrible odds, while others have failed even though they seemed to have everything in their favor Is it just luck? Or are there hidden clues that allow some investors to understand their risks and navigate around them to accomplish their goals?

WHAT IS DUE DILIGENCE?

Our first attraction to a business is often an attraction to the product itself. The gadget attracts us. "Wow! What a great idea! They'll sell millions of these!" This is when we start to look beyond the product and begin to ask questions about the business that produces and sells it. We understand the value of the product. Next we also need to understand the value of the business behind the product.

The businesses worth investing in are the sustainable businesses that are revenue based, product driven, and supported by an infrastructure that has been designed to sustain the business's long-term growth. These are the businesses that have real products and intellectual property and that have the ability to consistently deliver products profitably into the future. These are the sustainable businesses that are worth investing in.

The trick, of course, just as it was with the Edison Electric Light Company, is to identify whether a business is worth the commitment of investment funds. To know that you need to assess its ability to deliver a product and fulfill its customer orders while making a profit—and to repeat this over and over again. Putting the businesses luck and good timing aside, how do you assess a business to determine if it is sustainable and has the ability to succeed and grow over the long term? You do so using an assessment process known as due diligence.

Figure 1.1 Three Due Diligence Facets of a Business

Due diligence is a voyage of discovery. It is a process for searching beyond the products and venturing, by analysis and assessment, through three distinct facets of the business—its financial, legal, and operations frameworks—to discover clues for predicting its long-term sustainability (Figure 1.1).

The due diligence process will help you discover any unknown risks or opportunities that might exist for the investor. Each of the three facets represents a separate view of the business, and each must be assessed to determine the true value of the business prior to investing.

In many cases investors conduct their due diligence by bringing in only attorneys and financial auditors to perform assessments of the legal and financial facets of the business. No person or group is identified that is specifically tasked with or capable of performing a detailed assessment of the operations facet of the business. Occasionally an engineer may be asked to look at the product design, or a programmer may be asked to look at the software source code, and this evaluation of the product is then accepted as a valid analysis of the operations of the business. But these specialists do not take the whole operations context into their consideration.

The assessments of the legal and financial facets of the business are founded on the well-established principles of law and accounting, but there is no established method available to support an assessment of the operations facet that forms the backbone of a business. An operations assessment method would require probing a business's operations infrastructure to discover its ability to sustain its operations over time.

All businesses operate differently. Some operate by following deliberate planned and controlled processes, and some operate in an ad hoc manner, taking actions day by day as needs arise.

By assessing the operations facet of a business, investors are able to identify the latent risks and potential opportunities that could affect its future operations and to gain insight into the alignment of the business with their investment goals.

Financial Due Diligence

Financial due diligence is performed to assess the financial facet of a business. It is not used to assess the reasons behind the past performance of a business or the operational procedures used to support its future operations. Instead, the goal of financial due diligence is to establish a true current valuation for the business. It is an assessment of the financial position of the business at a point (usually its current position) in the continuum of its operations.

Financial due diligence, for instance, might indicate that the business had exceeded its sales goals for the last two years. How did it accomplish this? Did the market improve? Or did the company's sales process cause the business to improperly project sales (possibly to make the books look better)?

The financial infrastructure of a business is part of its operations infrastructure. Therefore, Operations Due Diligence includes an assessment of the continuing financial operations of the business rather than an assessment limited to just the business's current financial status. Care should be used to not confuse these activities:

- Financial due diligence is an assessment of the current financial position of the business.
- Operations Due Diligence includes an assessment of the financial infrastructure and continuing financial operations of the business.

Chapter 10 discusses the assessment of the financial operations infrastructure.

Financial due diligence is the domain of financial analysts and CPAs who look at financial documents like income statements and balance sheets to establish a value for the business. There have been many books written describing methods for conducting an effective financial due diligence.

Nothing presented in *Operations Due Diligence* is intended to remove or diminish your need to conduct a full financial due diligence including an audit by a competent and independent CPA.

Legal Due Diligence

Legal due diligence is performed to assess the legal facet of the business. The goal of legal due diligence is to explore the current legal status of the business, including any outstanding issues of ownership, pending legal actions, outstanding judgments, liabilities, employee actions, insurance claims, intellectual property (IP) rights, government limitations, certifications, and professional licenses.

The legal due diligence team is often used to support the investment transaction itself by preparing the transaction documents, resolving any issues involving the business's contract status, and preparing any required acquisition novations (replacements) of third-party contracts. Legal due diligence should be extensive and should identify all legal liabilities that might exist for the investor. You must have a very clear understanding of and insight into any legal risks you are assuming from an existing business.

Legal due diligence includes a review of any agreements that could limit or constrain the future operations of the business. The business has a legal requirement to disclose any and all existing, pending, or potential legal constraints that could restrict its future operations. Strategic partnership agreements, royalty agreements, vendor or reseller agreements, existing nondisclosure agreements, and labor agreements are examples of the types of constraints that must also be disclosed. Furthermore, the assignment of these agreements to new owners must also be considered.

The legal infrastructure of a business is part of its operations infrastructure. Operations Due Diligence therefore includes an assessment of the continuing legal operations of the business. Care should be used to not confuse these activities:

- Legal due diligence is an assessment of the current legal position of the business.
- Operations due diligence includes an assessment of the legal infrastructure and continuing legal operations of the business.

Chapter 11 discusses the assessment of the legal operations infrastructure.

Legal due diligence is the domain of attorneys who are responsible for determining the current legal commitments and status of the business.

Nothing presented in *Operations Due Diligence* is intended to remove or diminish your need to conduct a full legal due diligence with a competent attorney.

Operations Due Diligence

The 1990s saw the rise and fall of the dot-com businesses. These were the gee-wiz businesses with the flashy websites that were going to (and to a great extent did) revolutionize the way we do business. But the dot-coms—the virtual businesses whose main goal seemed to be raising investment dollars rather than delivering products, with a few exceptions—represented high-risk investments and didn't succeed well. They turned out to be far more risky than their investors had predicted. After consuming millions of investment dollars, the dot-com businesses found themselves suddenly being measured in the same way all other businesses have been historically measured: on their profits earned rather than their profits promised.

The question we can now ask is this: If investors had looked beyond the façade and understood the potential risks, would they have realized how many of the dot-com businesses did not actually represent a real opportunity? Would investors have realized that the dot-coms did not have the ability to produce the products required to make the projected (and needed) returns to sustain their operations?

Some of the dot-com businesses did succeed. And over time other Internet-based businesses, including names like Yahoo!, eBay, and Amazon.com, became highly successful. The investors in these businesses did well because they got smarter and started to look beyond the promises and began looking at the long-term sustainability of the businesses. The businesses that survived did so because they were committed as much to developing their operations infrastructure as they were to developing their products.

The businesses that continually improved their infrastructure by identifying and mitigating operational risks improved their sustainability and increased their odds of survival. As investors began to understand the importance of assessing the operational infrastructure in terms of the risks presented by the dot-com businesses, they were better able to mitigate their risks and improve the sustainability of the businesses. New web-based businesses continue to emerge and evolve today. It remains to be seen whether they have learned the lessons of the recent past.

And what about the risks and opportunities offered by the Old Economy businesses that have been operating successfully for years? Is a company's age an indicator of its future success? Many Old Economy businesses with long histories of success have also failed as new markets have evolved. Many continue to fail today because they are unable to remain profitable without retooling their operations from the methods that had sustained them in the past.

Many businesses with great product ideas struggle to develop the supporting infrastructure needed to bring these ideas along the entire path from concept to production. Businesses mature their operations with varying degrees of success. They know what product they want to bring to market, but they struggle when it comes to actually getting it there. Some businesses design their operations infrastructure in great detail, but others let their infrastructure evolve almost as an afterthought as the business grows and new needs arise. The latter is often called *organic growth*.

The goal of Operations Due Diligence is to allow an investor to determine the maturity of the business's operations infrastructure. Operations Due Diligence assesses the entire organization to determine how efficiently and effectively the business operates and to identify opportunities for improvement.

When asked how they will use this investment, many businesses reply with a shopping list in the form of a spend plan, which may address immediate needs but does not address the sustainability needs of the business. The questions that should be asked instead are these: What opportunities will you be able to capture if you receive this investment? How will you improve your operations infrastructure to ensure that these opportunities are realized?

Your assessment will determine whether the business has proactively designed its operations infrastructure with deliberation and intent or whether it has allowed its infrastructure to evolve organically in response to events. It's not unusual for a business to suffer growing pains when its growth outpaces its ability to hire qualified staff or to develop its operations infrastructure. However, the better route is for a business to develop a road map for growth, and it should have a plan for developing its infrastructure along with its products.

Due diligence should assess all three facets of a business. Conducting an effective due diligence requires performing a full Operations Due Diligence along with a legal and financial due diligence. It's important to keep in mind that due diligence is not a perfect science, and there is always the chance that your assessment will miss something. This book is a guide that will help you conduct an effective Operations Due Diligence. It's like a treasure map that shows you where to look. But the map is only your starting point. You still need to dig to find the treasure!

Whether it's an Old Economy, brick-and-mortar business or a virtual online business, whether it's a technology business or a service business, you need to perform financial and legal due diligence to determine the current status of the business. And you need to conduct a full Operations Due Diligence to ensure that you're investing in a business capable of sustaining its operations into the future.

SELF-ASSESSMENT AS A MANAGEMENT TOOL

With the economic recession of 2008, the finances of many long-established businesses became stressed, and they were no longer able to operate profitably. In some instances, the government went to their aid with financial support in an attempt to save jobs and rescue the failing economy. Financial help alone though may not have been the answer. The U.S. automobile industry was directly impacted by the downturn when the sudden lack of credit for buyers to purchase automobiles forced the market to shrink rapidly. With fewer cars being sold, buyers became more selective, and some of the automobile manufacturers were no longer able to compete. These businesses may have been destined to fail even without this economic stress because they had not updated their operations infrastructure and were already struggling to compete in a global market when the downturn occurred.

Supporting the U.S. automobile manufacturers may have been like returning a sick animal to the herd rather than curing it. The automobile manufacturers were able to survive with the infusion of capital from the government; however, without changing the way they operated, their demise might have only been delayed. To become sustainable, the operations of the U.S.

automakers had to evolve to allow them to compete with the foreign manufacturers that have been overtaking their industry. Their sales and marketing infrastructure needed to become more responsive as the market moved to new technologies such as hybrid cars; their personnel infrastructure needed to overcome the expensive salaries and benefits of their past organized labor agreements; and their production infrastructure needed to be able to support evolving manufacturing technologies.

The U.S. government and the American people became investors in these businesses when they supplied the capital that helped them survive. Since the government itself is not known for efficient operations, it was left to the automakers to self-assess their operations and determine what operational risks existed. Were they able to identify the root causes of their problems? Or did they rely solely on market pressure and politics to impose change on their infrastructure?

How well did automakers succeed? I guess time will tell. We'll just have to wait and see.

For most investors, a time-will-tell or wait-and-see approach means taking a huge risk. Most investors aren't willing to take this type of wait-and-see approach. Investors use the due diligence process to expose their risks early. Businesses, on the other hand, often hesitate to perform periodic self-assessments. They hesitate because they see the time and cost for performing a self-assessment as disruptive to their operations and expensive. They choose instead to "wait and see" rather than conduct a real self-assessment. In some instances managers may fear that publishing the results of a self-assessment could impact their jobs. As a result, the business fails to recognize or mitigate operations risks or take action to capture potential opportunities in a timely manner. "Our operations seem fine. . . . Let's wait and see what happens!"

> Risks that are not mitigated today become problems that need to be resolved tomorrow.

Operations Due Diligence, if undertaken internally, can be used as a management self-assessment tool and a means of proactively assessing operations risk and prioritizing future infrastructure improvements.

An operations assessment, whether performed as part of a due diligence or used as an internal management tool, is an exploration of the latent risks and opportunities that exist within the operations infrastructure of a business. Risks that are not mitigated today become problems that need to be resolved tomorrow. Operations assessments are performed to discover any existing conditions that might impact the sustainability of the business.

Unless a business proactively assesses its risks, it can fail to anticipate events like sudden changes in the market. The result can be that it fails to adjust its strategic plans in time to deliver products that continue to sell. The better answer would be to perform a self-assessment that allows the business to identify its risks and opportunities sooner, allowing risk mitigation and opportunity capture plans to be implemented in time to remain current with changes in the market.

The questions provided in Part Two can be used as a checklist to support an internal self-assessment. Performing a self-assessment enables managers to strengthen their business and help position it for a future investment event. Managers who run their business as if it is always for sale are constantly trying to maximize its value for investors. By assessing their own operations, managers are able to identify areas with latent risks and opportunities, and they can use this information to prioritize limited resources to target their process improvement needs. If managers perform internal assessments on a periodic basis, they will be able to use the results as a benchmark to measure their progress over time. Managers concerned about their jobs can use this as evidence of their personal performance and also to defend the expense of a self-assessment in their next budget.

On occasion, it is useful to have employees conduct an assessment independently from the management team. The contrast between the managers' view of the business and the employees' view of the business can be a springboard for an employee-sponsored, bottom-up continuous process improvement program.

When employees are asked to participate in the assessment, they must be made aware of the need for change so that they are less likely to resist the changes. Business operations areas about which employees and managers have significant differences in perception should become high-priority areas for future improvements. Managers who think everything is going fine might discover some serious risk areas using this method because employees are often in a better position than managers to spot improvement opportunities. Another approach to gaining efficient and honest insight is to contract the assessment to an independent, external team.

> Operations Due Diligence may be conducted more efficiently and honestly if it is contracted to an independent, external consulting team.

Throughout *Operations Due Diligence,* I refer generically to "investors." Generally, I am directly addressing readers who are involved with business mergers or acquisitions. But the term *investor* can also have additional meanings. Investing one's time, sweat, and energy in a business makes managers stakeholders in the business, and therefore they are making a personal investment. The managers of a business are also investing their professional reputation on the success of the business. By performing an internal due diligence, they will be challenging both themselves and the business to succeed.

HOW DO YOU SCORE THE ASSESSMENT QUESTIONS?

Part Two provides 400 operations assessment questions. Rather than simply providing a list of questions for the reader, each question in *Operations Due Diligence* is described in historic context intended to help the reader understand and retain the information. Operations questions are situational, and this approach was taken to help the reader understand and experience situations in which the question would apply. By providing context for the questions, you will be gaining experience that you can apply when you assess the due diligence responses you receive. This will help you better understand the question so that you are in a position to explore the answers and make better decisions about the sustainability of the business.

A summary of the assessment questions is provided at the end of each chapter in Part Two. These questions can be compiled into a worksheet to support your assessments. If a question doesn't seem relevant to your business, before discounting it, you should challenge yourself to answer it or consider why it's not relevant for this business.

There is a tendency to ask what the correct or acceptable answers to these questions are. There is no one correct answer. The answers depend on your investment goals. The assessment questions are not intended to be used as a test that can be passed or failed. An Operations Due Diligence is an exploration through which you hope to discover any investment risks and opportunities. You are trying to establish a true, correct view of the business. The correct answers to these questions will depend on your investment strategy, the risk you are willing to take, the opportunities you are hoping to capture, and your expectations for the near-term and long-term plans for growing the business.

> Operations Due Diligence should *not* be looked at as a test that has a passing grade. The correct answers depend on achieving a balance between the risk the investor is willing to take and the opportunities the business offers.

And the next thing you will logically ask is this: What is an acceptable score when the results of the questions are compiled or added up? There are no perfect answers to any of these questions, nor is there some magic score that will guarantee a successful investment in a business. The goal of an Operations Due Diligence is to allow you to enter into an investment with as much knowledge about the business as possible.

By performing an Operations Due Diligence, you hope to discover where the weaknesses and strengths of the business may exist. From this you will be able to identify areas where additional work is needed to improve and grow the business. If your investment strategy is to discover opportunities to improve the business by identifying its existing weaknesses, then this assessment will disclose where those opportunities might exist. For example, if you identify that the business has a weak sales organization, then your investment plans might be to create an opportunity by putting additional funds into the sales organization after the acquisition. If you anticipate making a one-time investment in the business, then this may not be a good opportunity because it doesn't align with your investment goals. If the acquisition is expected to be your first step and you anticipate making a continuing investment and long-term improvement in the business, then this may be the opportunity you are looking for and the operations assessment has identified the need to prioritize your investment in the sales organization.

Operations Due Diligence will tell you how well the business aligns with your investment plans. There's no such thing as a perfect operations assessment score because investors are all looking for different things.

In some cultures, the word for risk and the word for opportunity are the same. You need to decide for yourself whether the balance between the investment risk and the potential opportunities is acceptable based on your own investment goals. Operations Due Diligence is a subjective assessment that is guided by the needs and intentions of the investor. Your assessment of the responses will require a judgment call on your part based on your knowledge of the investment plan. This makes the generation of any kind of meaningful standardized score for the assessment impossible. It is more important that you understand the nature of the questions in order to make these judgments, . . . which is why I have chosen this format for *Operations Due Diligence.*

The questions in *Operations Due Diligence* may seem arbitrary. There may seem to be a simple or obvious answer. The question might lead to a more complex discussion, however. For instance, one of the questions regarding customer satisfaction is this: "Has the product been released too soon?" Simply asking a business this question will likely be answered with a swift "No." The question is intended to be an indicator of latent product quality risks so it is an important question that allows the assessment team to explore product maturity in detail. It is your job to determine when a sufficient answer has been received, and not simply parrot the business's responses. In this case, in order to properly answer the question, you may need to ask employees and customers about the quality of the product or look at test logs. When the business answers a question one way and your assessment answers it a different way, you will need to determine whether the business is being intentionally misleading or if it simply misunderstood the intent of the question.

THE BS QUOTIENT

Because Operations Due Diligence relies on a broad range of disciplines rather than a specific or well-established method such as exists in accounting and law, there is much more room for creative responses to your questions. The answers to assessment questions will be understandably biased toward the business and tend to give the answer the person being questioned thinks the assessor wants to hear.

Operations Due Diligence requires an on-site assessment, which can become a time for the business to cleverly hide its scars and emphasize the positives rather than being forthright about the weaknesses that might exist. This happens because the business may not understand that identifying weak areas is exactly where the investor will see opportunities and justification for an investment.

Continuing the prior example: If the business has a regional sales organization, expanding this group could be an opportunity to greatly improve the performance of the business, and this might be exactly what an investor is looking for. A strategy that leverages the parent business's existing national sales team and broadens the market for its products is a common investment strategy. By not disclosing that the existing sales team is regional for fear it will be seen as a weakness, the investor might not recognize that an opportunity exists. It's your job to find the unrecognized potentials in a business by probing past the stars in the managers' eyes when they say things like "Those forecasts are really very conservative." Or "We can't help but exceed these estimates next year."

One of the cautions I use throughout *Operations Due Diligence* is to watch for the "BS Quotient." I make no claims to the originality of this term, but the explanation I offer for the term "BS Quotient" is as follows: It was believed by some of my Irish ancestors that kissing the Blarney Stone (BS) could make a person . . . something less than honest. Of course, my ancestors would never tell an out-and-out lie, but they were occasionally known to stretch the truth . . . a wee bit. How often a person was suspected of kissing the Blarney Stone led to a factor of believability in their stories that I refer to here as the BS Quotient! The more a person kissed the stone, the higher his or her BS Quotient was and the further he or she might be expected to stretch the truth. There are other meanings also associated with the term "BS," but I assure you, I associate BS with the myth of the Blarney Stone. Call it as you like. My caution to watch the BS Quotient is also stated as "Let the buyer beware." A good sales team knows just how to attain the correct BS Quotient, and it will be your job to recognize it during the due diligence.

The following is an example of stretching the truth by increasing the BS Quotient. While both of the following statements are true, they have two very different meanings:

We expect to sell 45,000 of these units this month.
We have orders for 45,000 of these units this month.

The BS Quotient is clearly higher in the first statement.

Your goal is to try to get the BS Quotient to zero. The following are further examples of statements that have different BS Quotient levels. You must learn to sort through them to find the truth. Listen to the differences in the following statements:

I believe it will be ready by next month.
That product will be released in 30 days.

Look out for the "I believe" and "I expect" statement in any form. Whenever you hear "I believe" or "I expect," a bell should go off in your head to ask more questions. Your job is to find out what the facts really are, not what someone "believes" they are. That is, unless of course you are relying on their expert opinion.

The next set of statements are very common in both large and small businesses, and they represent an area where particular attention should be paid as it may give some insights into the true ethics of the business:

We use the latest versions for all of our software development tools.
All of our development tools are fully licensed.

Do you recognize the underlying BS in the first statement? Many businesses use the latest tools, but the tools are not legally licensed. They are copied from another source, which is a huge risk. You need to challenge the answers you receive if they leave room for or imply a potential risk. Using the latest versions is a good thing. It is an ethical issue if the software hasn't been licensed and a liability risk for an investor.

The next set of statements goes right to the heart of the business. Policies and procedures can be the manifestation of the operations infrastructure of the business and they can define how the operations are conducted. Or they can sit on the shelf and be used only as a method for establishing human resource boundaries:

We have a policies and procedures manual.
We follow defined processes and have an active process improvement
     group.

Yes, you have a policies and procedures manual, but do your employees have a copy of it, and have they been trained in the procedures, and is there an ongoing effort to improve on the procedures that the employees participate in? The BS Quotient is much higher in the first statement.

It is important to look for and understand the BS Quotient and to let the business know you are looking for it. Challenging some of the responses and letting the business know that you are attuned to this possibility at an early point in the assessment will make your job much easier in the long run. One way to help this along is to respond to answers by asking a simple question: "Can you show me evidence of that?"

CHAPTER 2

The Due Diligence Process

Early in the seventeenth century, as exploration and settlement of the New World was beginning to expand, Spain sent large fleets of wooden ships to the New World in search of silver and gold. As these wooden ships traveled the shores of the Americas on their return trips to Spain, they were often overloaded with treasure, even replacing their ballast stones with gold in order to steady the frail vessels and allow them to carry more of the precious cargo. These ships frequently became the victims of wind and weather, and entire fleets of them sank at the hands of Florida's notorious hurricanes.

For centuries afterward, these ships became the focus of intensive searches by treasure hunters hoping to recover their lost bounty. Some treasure was found by a lucky few who happened to be in the right place at the right time and happened to stumble onto it. One of the greatest treasures to be recovered to date, worth millions of dollars, was discovered by a treasure hunter named Mel Fisher. Some of the treasure he found is maintained today by the Mel Fisher Museum in Florida. Fisher discovered a Spanish galleon named the *Atocha* located 20 miles off the coast of Key West, Florida. His discovery wasn't all luck. He had searched and studied for years in order to determine the location of the *Atocha* wreck site. Mel Fisher had done his homework and had correctly identified the area to search in.

You will also need to do your homework in preparation for an Operations Due Diligence. Conducting a well-planned assessment will yield far better results than merely hoping to stumble upon the correct answers.

Operations Due Diligence is a guide to help you conduct an effective assessment. It can be used to help develop your due diligence strategy, which will become the "treasure map" you'll follow.

The strategy you plan and ultimately implement will be constrained by your timeline and schedule. It took Mel Fisher years of research to discover the location of the *Atocha* wreck site. Most assessment teams are lucky to get even a couple of weeks to research and plan.

Mel Fisher (August 21, 1922–December 19, 1998) was an American treasure hunter best known for finding the wreck of the Spanish galleon *Nuestra Señora de Atocha*. He discovered the wreck July 20, 1985. The estimated $450 million cache recovered, known as "The *Atocha* Motherlode," included 40 tons of gold and silver and some 100,000 Spanish silver coins known as "pieces of eight," gold coins, Colombian emeralds, gold and silver artifacts, and 1,000 silver bars. Large as it was, this was only roughly half of the treasure that went down with the *Atocha*. Still missing are 300 silver bars and eight bronze cannons, among other things. (See the Mel Fisher Museum, melfisher.org/museum.)

This book provides a systematic method for conducting an Operations Due Diligence. As with other business processes, where there is a need for repeatability and consistently reliable results, the due diligence process itself needs to be institutionalized and improved over time.

Due diligence is usually conducted by a team working for investors (or internally for management). The investors in these cases may not play a direct role in the assessment, but they need to provide specific direction to the team about their investment goals. Whether Operations Due Diligence is performed by an external or internal team, the process is the same. It's an assessment of the operations infrastructure of a business, which will be used to identify latent risks and opportunities so that you can plan for the future growth and sustainability of the business.

There are three distinct phases to the Operations Due Diligence process (see Figure 2.1): the first phase is the preparation, which I refer to as *planning for discovery*; the second phase is the on-site assessment; and the final phase is the assessment report.

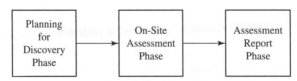

Figure 2.1 The Due Diligence Process

Each phase has distinct activities that need to be performed and should not be skipped. The assessment team must be allowed the time to systematically complete each phase. If you rush to accomplish the second phase, the on-site assessment, before fully completing the first phase, planning for discovery, you'll very likely waste your own time as well as the business's and you'll also likely miss opportunities for valid discovery. Planning and conducting the Operations Due Diligence is not enough though. After completing the on-site assessment, the results must be collected and analyzed during the third phase, the assessment report.

PLANNING FOR DISCOVERY

Operations Due Diligence is a discovery process. You need to have a map, and you better do your homework!

The planning for discovery phase is designed to give you early insight into the business and its markets. You will use the information gathered here to plan your strategy for further exploration during the on-site assessment phase. This will allow you to prioritize your exploration and determine which assessment areas you need to explore in further detail. Your strategy should be to plan greater disclosure in the areas you foresee the greatest risks or opportunities. It's critical therefore that you have taken the time to establish your investment goals in advance: Is this a strategic acquisition? Are you looking for a bargain basement purchase that can be made profitable with an infusion of new capital? Is there some buried intellectual property that's being sought? Understanding the goals of the acquisition will help focus your search.

If this is an internal assessment, managers need to establish clear goals for the internal assessment team by setting boundaries on the scope of the assessment. Are you assessing the entire operations infrastructure of the business or only an area where you anticipate risk? Rather than assessing all areas (see Chapter 3) at once, you might decide that it's less disruptive to restrict the assessment to one area at a time.

The assessment team represents the investors, and it is typically treated very well when on site. I know of a case in which the due diligence team members were wined and dined so well they barely had a chance to show up for the assessment or to ask the hard questions they should have been asking! The assessment team must remain focused on its task.

The Operations Due Diligence plan can be as simple as creating an agenda that clearly lays out the areas to be explored, the documents to be requested, and the people to be interviewed, or it can be as complex as creating a multimonth schedule with a list of requested appointments. The agenda should leave plenty of room for expansion. As questions are asked and employees are interviewed, more questions will arise, as will additional names to be interviewed. The treasure is not always found lying on the bottom in clear sight. Sometimes you have to dig around in the mud a little to find the gold! Plan your exploration accordingly.

Your Operations Due Diligence plan needs to identify any specialized skills needed by the assessment team. Will you need to look at software source code or other areas requiring engineering specialization? If so, people who have these skills need to be identified and included as members of the assessment team, and they need to be trained how to perform a due diligence.

A meeting of the assessment team should be held prior to going on site to ensure that individual team members understand their roles, what is expected of them, and the goals of the team. Schedules need to be emphasized, and the team lead should have an established action item management plan in place to coordinate further team activities and follow-up. Expectations of team conduct must be clearly explained. For instance, all team members are bound by the nondisclosure agreement, and the terms of this agreement should be fully explained to the entire team. In some situations, individual nondisclosure agreements may also be asked for when contractors or consultants are used to supplement the skills of the team.

The treasure is not always found lying on the bottom in clear sight. Sometimes you have to dig around in the mud a little to find the gold!

Each chapter in Part Two presents a list of assessment questions. Each question is placed in context so that the reader will understand its relevance. As each question is answered, it exposes additional information about the business potentially revealing additional latent operations risks and potential opportunities. The questions are tools that guide the assessment team through the discovery process. Each question is designed to expose a potential weakness that could imply an operational risk for the business. For instance, one of the questions from Chapter 9 is, "Does the business follow a documented staffing policy?" If the answer to this question is no, it could indicate a weakness and reveal a potential risk. With this weakness, the business might be liable for an employment lawsuit, might not properly identify the skills needed to develop a product, or might be overpaying salaries. Each of these has the potential to impact the sustainability of the business and therefore is a risk that should be mitigated (by creating a formalized staffing policy).

NONDISCLOSURE AGREEMENTS

A *nondisclosure agreement* (NDA) should be the first agreement put in place between the parties of any investment event. Not all investors agree with this, however. Many investors, including some very reputable venture companies, take the position that they are in the business of looking at businesses and an NDA would be needlessly constraining to them. In these situations, the business needs to determine the extent of the risk they are willing to take. It may be obvious, but it's worth stating here: Not all due diligence is conducted by earnest buyers and investors. Strategic buyers are often competitors who are trying to capture additional market share. There are lots of sharks in the venture capital ocean waiting to gobble up unsuspecting businesses. It's a good practice for a business to perform its own due diligence on potential investors who could become its future partners.

Allowing a competitor to perform a detailed due diligence is a very risky step for any business to take, but it is one that may be absolutely necessary if you are looking for a strategic buyer for your business. Strategic buyers are often incentivized to pay a higher price than nonstrategic buyers would because they are eliminating a competitor and increasing their market share. The problem is for the targeted business to determine whether the competitor is looking seriously at an acquisition or just using the due diligence as an opportunity to gain insight into its competition and the market. Some businesses have used this less-than-ethical approach when trying to capture intelligence about another business's products, methods, financials, pricing, and so on. The Operations Due Diligence process makes all of this information available to a competitor, and it even enables the competitor to challenge the business for its decision rationale so the competitor can understand the business's strategic thinking. The due diligence team needs to be sensitive to this and understand that hesitation on the part of the business to provide information may be well justified.

Most businesses understand that it's difficult to avoid this type of unethical activity when inviting a due diligence, and therefore they will take steps to legally protect themselves as much as possible. The letter of intent and the mutual nondisclosure agreement between the parties should address directly the need of both parties to be earnest, to limit access to due diligence data, and to agree that the information obtained is to be used solely for the purpose of the acquisition or investment. A qualified attorney should always be used to prepare and review due diligence confidentiality documents.

> Not all due diligence assessments are conducted by earnest buyers and investors.

Ethical conduct can be an issue for an internal due diligence as well. When employees are appointed to an internal assessment team, they may have access to information that is outside the scope of their normal work environment. As a minimum, you need to be able to trust them with confidential information, and they should understand the need to maintain the confidentiality of the data they are allowed to access. Instructions to assessment team members should include the following statement: "During the internal due diligence you may have access to the payroll database, but you may not discuss this to information or use it for any purpose beyond the scope of the assessment."

ON-SITE ASSESSMENTS

If the due diligence process were a "journey of discovery," then the on-site assessment phase would be "dealing with the native population"! The on-site assessment should follow a strict agenda, which you will have prepared during the planning for discovery phase. You will have provided the agenda to the business in advance of the on-site assessment, and you will have established a single point of contact that you will be able to work through.

The business will need to collect any requested documentation in advance, along with any records or other data requested (by either copying the documents or loading them electronically into a due diligence document management system). Receipts should be provided for all documents collected, and they should all be covered by the NDA.

There are no rules for how long the on-site assessment should take. The investors establish the schedule and timeline, and you don't want to be rushed. You'll need enough time to be thorough, but you must always try to minimize your disruption of the operations of the business. There may be a lot riding on your analysis, and you'll want to make good use of your time. The more complete you are when doing your homework during the planning for discovery phase, the more thorough—not quicker—you'll be when performing your assessment. The more you can inform the business's managers about your expectations for the on-site assessment phase, the better prepared they will be and the quicker you will be able to complete the assessment. Sending the business a list of needed documents and staff members you want to interview in advance will be a big time saver.

If the business managers are speaking with multiple investors, they will often maintain a file of due diligence documents, prepared in advance, in anticipation of the questions they expect to be asked (or have already been asked by others). They may also attempt to avoid some questions or exclude some documents from the file that could disclose a known problem (negative findings from customer surveys or product defect reports, for instance) in hopes that the due diligence team will overlook a potential problem. Why shine a spotlight on a known problem, right? For this reason, your assessment shouldn't be limited to an existing due diligence file, and you should feel free to make any requests you deem necessary. It's your job to lead the assessment, and this is your event, so request any additional data you feel you need, and don't rely strictly on the view of the business that its managers want you to see.

You should consider the due diligence data the business provides as only the beginning of your exploration. You will have to continue to dig for evidence to validate what you find in the file. In order to get a true picture of the business, you will need to get below the surface and start digging around in the mud! The questions provided in this book may be only the starting point for your exploration.

All of the questions in *Operations Due Diligence* are summarized at the end of each chapter, making them easy to use to create your own work-sheets. One of the comments I hear regularly is, "That's a lot of questions. Do I need to ask all of them?" My response is, "No, but if you're putting seven figures into the deal, you might want to take the time." For the pur-poses of this book, I felt it was better to provide too many questions than too few. As you conduct your due diligence, you may decide not to use the entire list. This is your decision, which will depend on your needs and the areas on which you want to focus your exploration.

You can either use the questions "as is," or you can use them as a start-ing point and make modifications to your worksheet to meet your own needs.

Do these questions cover every possible nuance of a business? Probably not! All businesses are different, and, again, you are encouraged to modify the questions based on your own investment goals and needs. If you feel that some of the questions don't apply to the business you are assessing, I encourage you to identify a clear rationale for why they don't apply before you drop them. Rather than just dropping a question, try modifying it first so that it better fits the business. You'll have to use some judgment when modifying or creating your own list of questions.

Furthermore, if you drop questions for expedience or because of time constraints, I suggest you do so only following the planning for discovery phase and after giving consideration to the depth of exploration you feel you will need in each area. This is a discovery process, and it's not always possible to predict what path your discovery might take.

You will use the questions presented in Part Two during the on-site assessment. As an alternate approach and to save time, you can send the questions to the business in advance and ask the managers to respond to the questions in writing in advance. In these situations, the on-site assessment is used to validate the answers and to further explore questionable answers. This approach also has the advantage of having the business managers document their responses, which can prove useful if there are any problems in the future: "During due diligence you said the software had been released, but it's clear it hadn't been tested as required by your quality assurance (QA) plan."

If you've done your homework during the planning for discovery phase, you will have a good idea of what to look for and where to search during the on-site assessment. You'll have a plan that supports your investment strategy, and the result will be that you'll gain more insight and efficiency during your on-site assessment. Your on-site assessment will have a greater chance of discovering potential areas of risk or opportunity, and you'll be ready to probe deeper into problem areas based on the responses you receive.

The on-site assessment is your opportunity to experience the business firsthand, to observe its operations across the organization, and to meet and get to know the staff members at a working level. Critical items like team dynamics are better understood through observation than through organization charts.

The due diligence data you collect will take on many forms. The Appendix includes a generalized list of documents to be requested. These documents are the operational evidence that backs up the responses you receive. You will want to expand and amend the list as needed. It is not necessary to review these documents while you are on site if the business is willing to allow you to have remote access to them. Requesting these documents in an electronic, searchable format and reviewing them in advance will allow you to spend less time on site. It will also allow you time during the on-site assessment to be more targeted, enabling you to verify rather than collect the requisite data and information.

You need to protect the confidentiality of the assessment data and often the confidentiality of the event itself. This is particularly true if one of the parties to the deal is a public entity. The employees of the business may not know that the business is for sale, or they may not understand the role new investors will be taking. Collecting documents and other forms of data, at the detailed level needed for Operations Due Diligence, while maintaining a high level of confidentiality is a concern for both parties. The parties should agree early on what the timing will be for when a potential acquisition will occur and when it will be exposed to the employees.

Employees will wonder why their working documents are being collected, which can easily result in a panicked staff at a time when stability is critical. If the deal is explained initially simply as a new investment, it will often help to eliminate employee concerns.

VIRTUAL DEAL ROOMS

A *virtual deal room* (VDR) is an electronic form of the due diligence file. With the availability of low-priced scanners, document-imaging software, and cloud servers, the traditional due diligence document file box has quickly been replaced by technology. Managing the due diligence documents electronically offers a tremendous advantage over the past "box" method. All of the documents need to be in a text searchable form. Electronic documents come in many forms (different file types) including e-mails, and some of them may not be easily copied from their native format into the due diligence collection (for instance, they may require their native software application to be viewed). The file box method has been replaced by an online database with the collection of due diligence documents saved electronically. Virtual deal room software is now widely available on the market as are a wide range of document hosting services that allow you to search and view documents that have different file formats. VDR services also include the use of online document management tools that are provided by online hosting companies that offer a wide range of search and categorization capabilities to securely support remote users.

A document review can include thousands of paper and electronic documents. Collection, distribution, and collaboration for large numbers of documents can also require a large document review team to access the documents. In the past these reviewers were collected into a single location where document access and availability could be controlled. But today, with the advent of browser-based document management systems, reviewers can search and select documents from remote locations, even from their home. VDR systems, which allow all parties to have access to the due diligence documents remotely, are being used to overcome many of the problems of document management and control. More important, it typically costs less to set up a virtual deal room than to pay travel expenses and so on to establish a dedicated team of reviewers.

When collecting due diligence documents, some care has to be taken to identify the format of the data. Will documents be delivered in paper format, or will they be delivered electronically in Word or pdf format? The average lifespan of an electronic document is less than five years. After that, there is a good likelihood that the format of the native file (the software application used to create it) may have become outdated or obsolete as the technology used to create it has continued to evolve. Paper documents may in fact be better long-term alternatives to computer files, but paper is not electronically searchable. Remember that the native documents may have been created by word processors, spreadsheets, accounting systems, computer-assisted design (CAD) programs, or other software applications that are no longer available. "Yes, those projections were created for us by a vendor on an IBM 360, but we stopped using them years ago." As paper documents are scanned, they're also processed through an optical character recognition (OCR) tool that creates a computer searchable text file.

The question could be whether or not these systems are available to review the documents today and whether they will exist in the future if the document needs to be accessed. Converting the native files to a common format (generally a tif or pdf image) is a viable alternative that allows the document to be "petrified" in a common format for future reference. There are tools available that have been designed specifically to convert random file types to common file formats.

If one of the parties to the deal is a public company, there may also be regulatory and compliance rules that restrict how the deal is disclosed and how the document collection must be handled. A securities attorney should be consulted. In these cases you may need to provide document access audit trails that clearly identify who has had access to each of the due diligence documents.

> Care must also be taken if the data includes any form of personnel-related privacy-sensitive information.

Care must also be taken if the due diligence data includes any form of sensitive, private personnel information such as employee Social Security or health-care records. VDR systems are able to establish viewing privileges (not everyone generally needs to see all documents) and to track who has had access to which documents. Granting reviewers access to confidential data must be carefully controlled. These rules may apply to customer data as well as employee data. If the business retains customer records that are controlled by privacy laws such as HIPAA, all rules that apply to the business's handling of this data also apply to the due diligence team. (The Health Insurance Portability and Accountability Act, HIPAA, was enacted by the Congress in 1996.)

VDR systems offer a good alternative for controlling costs and limiting access to confidential data. They should not be used as an alternate to meeting with the staff members and observing the operations of the business. This is your opportunity to observe the employee team firsthand. Take advantage of the opportunity. The need for an on-site assessment is particularly important for observing the operations facet of the business. It may be possible to review the books and contracts for the legal and financial facets of the business remotely. It's not possible to observe the interactions and operations of the business remotely.

ASSESSMENT REPORTS

The final phase of the due diligence process is the assessment report phase (see Figure 2.1). The Operations Due Diligence is not performed to simply collect information about the business. During the assessment report phase, the data you previously collected needs to be analyzed to determine the level of latent operations risks and opportunities that could potentially affect the sustainability of the business.

Following the on-site assessment, you will need to diligently analyze, catalog, and report all of your findings. Using a format that will support an eventual investment decision, the assessment results will need to be described in the form of potential risks that need to be mitigated and opportunities that can be captured. The questions listed in Part Two may be used "as is" for your due diligence worksheet.

Some questions may require a simple yes or no answer. Others may be direct requests for data: "What is the longevity and average turnover rate of employees?" These types of questions require a very specific answer, and they should be responded to with the requested information. Whether the question requires a yes or no response or a specific data input, it is important to consider what the implied risk the response might indicate for the business. "Does the business have a written ethics policy?" If the answer is no, then there is clearly an implied risk for the business because it has not set standards for employee conduct.

The responses to some questions may leave room for more subjectivity. I use a very simple response method intended to be self-evident to a reviewer and provide an easy ranking:

☐ Don't know ☐ Weak area ☐ Work in progress ☐ Strong area ☐ N/A

Comment: _____

This type of response to subjective questions is preferred because it records your observations rather than requiring a numerical score to quantify the results, and it supports the categorization of the data rather than appearing like qualitative test answers.

Each of the questions provided in Part Two can potentially result in the identification of an existing risk or opportunity that would then be documented in a risks and opportunities report. Not all questions result in a risks and opportunities report, however. The comment field can be used to provide any notable details that were observed. The assessor's rationale for each answer should be provided in the comment field for all questions whether categorized as weak or strong. "Why did you rate this as a strong area?" The comments are then gathered up as input to your assessment report.

The risks and opportunities report form shown in Figure 2.2 should be used to document each risk or opportunity that the team discovers. Each risk or opportunity will require some action either to mitigate the risk or to capture the opportunity. Use these forms to support your investment decision or recommendations.

The assessment report consists of (1) a catalog list of the documents and data collected throughout the process; (2) the responses to the Operations Due Diligence assessment questions; (3) a list of all identified risks and opportunities; and (4) a summary of the analysis and findings.

<u>Risk/Opportunity Report Form</u>

Name of risk or opportunity: _____

Brief description of risk or opportunity:

Likelihood of occurrence (percent):

Mitigation or capture strategy:

Likelihood of occurrence after mitigation (percent):

<u>Check one of the boxes below:</u>

| Risk: | Technical ☐ | Cost ☐ | Sales ☐ | Schedule ☐ |
| Opportunity: | Technical ☐ | Cost ☐ | Sales ☐ | Schedule ☐ |

Figure 2.2 Example of a Risk/Opportunity Report Form

Figure 2.3 is an example of a response to one of the assessment questions with an associated risk/opportunity report. Note that the answers are short and highly focused. As an example, in performing the discovery related to this question, you had the opportunity to observe a limiting factor in the sales and marketing infrastructure of the business. You could have identified this factor as a risk. However, by identifying it as a potential opportunity due to some mitigating future activity that will be the result of the investors' working toward their own goals (expanding the existing sales territories), you have converted this potential risk into an opportunity with some investment. As a result of this report, you have now gained several things. You've discovered a very real situation that exists within the business. You have stated the facts as they exist, and you've suggested a capture strategy to seize the opportunity.

Would there have been a benefit to have given this question's answer a numeric score? Should the score have been a negative or a positive? The answer is this: If the investment strategy had included improvements to the sales infrastructure, then this situation could be seen as a positive (an opportunity to improve the business through investment); if not, it could be seen as a negative (an unanticipated cost to improve the sales infrastructure).

The role of the Operations Due Diligence report is to provide information about the business, not to make an investment recommendation. It provides information that is used to support an eventual investment decision. The goal is to ensure that investors have all the information they need

Business XYZ

1. Documents Collected
- Sales and marketing plan
- Monthly quota sheets for each territory
- Sales territory map

2. Questions and Answers
Are sales forecasts based on the use of historical benchmarks that have been derived from a repeatable process?

☐ Don't know   ☐ Weak area   ☑ Work in progress   ☐ Strong area   ☐ N/A

Comment: *While there are no defined processes for tracking sales estimates by territory, several territory managers discussed the ad hoc process they use as the basis of their projections. During these discussions we found out that they do in fact track these numbers from year to year. We also found that each salesperson was traveling 3 days a week on average to maintain his or her relationships with current customers while seeking residual product sales.*

Risk/Opportunity Report Form Example

Risk/Opportunity Report Form

Name of risk or opportunity: __*Existing sales force is saturated.*__

Brief description of risk or opportunity:
The current sales force is on the road almost continuously. While they are meeting their quotas, the constant travel is creating a morale issue, and they are not spending enough time identifying additional prospects.

Likelihood of occurrence (percent):
We spoke with 3 of the 4 territory managers and had similar answers from all of them. We are therefore estimating a 100% likelihood that there is an opportunity to improve sales.

Mitigation or capture strategy:
We observed that, while the territory sales managers were saturated (overloaded), overall they were happy with the company. By dividing their current territories and adding additional staff, it will be possible to maintain the level of sales from the territory managers, reduce their travel, and increase sales overall.

Likelihood of occurrence after mitigation (percent):
Less than 25% if there are new sales representatives for the existing territory manager.

Check one of the boxes below:

Risk:	Technical ☐	Cost ☐	Sales ☐	Schedule ☐
Opportunity:	Technical ☐	Cost ☐	Sales ☑	Schedule ☐

---

3. Summary of Analysis and Findings
In accordance with the investment plan, all of the risks identified during the Operations Due Diligence have reasonable mitigation plans, and there is a great likelihood of capturing some of the discovered opportunities.

Figure 2.3 Example of a Completed Risk/Opportunity Report Form

to make a valid decision that will support their investment strategy. The report makes the investors aware of any risks that could impact the sustainability of the business, and it tells them how much effort will be required to mitigate the risk. The report should also make the investors aware of any potential opportunities that might add additional value to their investment, and it should tell them what it will take to capture these opportunities.

If the report is the result of an internal operations assessment rather than the result of investors' due diligence, the risk and opportunity information should be used to support strategic planning and to help management prioritize limited infrastructure development resources. With the assessment results in hand, the business can proactively manage its risk and opportunity identification.

CHAPTER 3

Infrastructure Assessment Areas

The operations infrastructure is the backbone of any business. It integrates the processes, methods, and workflow that support the organizational transactions and forms the underlying framework guiding the way work is performed throughout the business. The operations infrastructure defines all of the methods the business will use. By continually searching for new ways to improve its infrastructure, the business is continually improving the way it operates, and the increases in efficiency will make it more profitable.

The operations infrastructure of a business is commonly confused with its organizational structure (that is, its organization chart). They are not the same things. The organizational structure is a component of the operations infrastructure. The structure defines what the elements of the business are but not how they operate. The organizational structure says there is an engineering department. The operations infrastructure defines how the engineering department operates and interacts with other departments.

Infrastructures, by their definition, cross organizational boundaries. Because businesses are all different, they do not all have the same functional structure. For example, some have a human resources (HR) department, and some do not. It is important to define the infrastructure by the work that is being performed rather than the organization that is doing the work. One business is not better than another business simply because of the way it defines its organizational structure. One business becomes better than the other because it performs work more efficiently.

OPERATIONS INFRASTRUCTURE AREAS

The term *operations infrastructure* is an inclusive term that spans and supports work as it progresses through all of the organizational functions of a business. Within *Operations Due Diligence*, I divide the operations

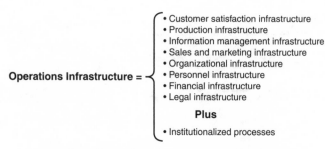

Figure 3.1 Operations Infrastructure Components

infrastructure into eight subinfrastructure areas plus the institutionalized processes that, in combination, support all of the work to be performed by a business (see Figure 3.1). These areas include the customer satisfaction, production, information management, sales and marketing, organizational, personnel, financial, and legal operating functions of the business plus all of the institutionalized processes and procedures that guide these operations. These subinfrastructure areas represent the major workflows that all businesses must accomplish.

Part Two describes each of the eight subinfrastructure areas plus the institutionalized processes that form the operations infrastructure and are core to any business. An Operations Due Diligence assesses the full cross-functional workflow, including the sales and marketing role in requirements analysis that should drive the design of a product. An assessment of the production infrastructure should include all workflow that crosses the entire organization and should not be limited to the "product side of the house" (engineering, manufacturing, and so on). The production infrastructure therefore also includes both the technical areas like the engineering department and the nontechnical areas like the sales department that support the definition of new product requirements.

The operations infrastructure includes the major workflows used by all businesses. Each of these areas must be continuously improved to grow and sustain the business if it is to remain competitive. Your Operations Due Diligence should assess these areas to determine how well the business has implemented its operations infrastructure. Did each area evolve organically over time, in an ad hoc manner as the business grew, or did each area evolve through planning and intent with the goal of supporting the future growth of the business and making it more competitive?

Each chapter in Part Two describes the assessment of one of the subinfrastructure areas. The final chapter describes the need for *institutionalizing the infrastructure* (that is, documenting and enforcing the policies and procedures) according to industry-defined methods, and it describes how to assess the institutional processes that support the subinfrastructure areas. The method chosen to institutionalize a business's infrastructure crosses all of the operations areas, and it is very much industry driven. The operations infrastructure assessment areas discussed in Part Two include the following:

Assessment of the customer satisfaction infrastructure (Chapter 4)
Assessment of the production infrastructure (Chapter 5)
Assessment of the information management infrastructure (Chapter 6)
Assessment of the sales and marketing infrastructure (Chapter 7)
Assessment of the organizational infrastructure (Chapter 8)
Assessment of the personnel infrastructure (Chapter 9)
Assessment of the financial infrastructure (Chapter 10)
Assessment of the legal infrastructure (Chapter 11)
Assessment of the institutionalized processes (Chapter 12)

It's common to hear that a due diligence has been performed to assess a specific functional area of a business. In these cases, an investor conducts a "management due diligence" or a "technical due diligence" with the goal of assessing only a portion of a business. Sometimes this means that the investor had ready access to an expert in one functional area or another or had some driving reason to be concerned about an individual area. Assessing an individual functional area is also a method used by managers who are having problems with an individual operations function. This could be an assessment of the sales and marketing function, for instance, if there were a problem with the sales pipeline and the assessment was to be used to find the root cause of the problem. A technical due diligence might include only an assessment of the product side of the house without considering the role other organizational functions play in the definition of a product. A true Operations Due Diligence should not be limited to a single operations function. Rather, it should have a broad scope that includes all of the operations areas.

OPERATIONS TRANSACTION POINTS

One of the goals of *Operations Due Diligence* is to help readers start thinking about a business in terms of its operations workflows rather than its department structures.

Focusing on workflow allows readers to start thinking about the way work is accomplished and forces readers to begin looking at the organizational transaction points that support workflow rather than being locked into a predetermined organizational structure. "How" work is performed is more important than "who" performs it for this discussion. We deal with "who" later in the book.

While there are no absolute right or wrong organizational structures, there are functions that all businesses employ in some manner. From our previous example, not all businesses have an HR department, but they must all deal with hiring employees, administering employee benefits, and so on. Therefore, they must all accomplish these HR functions in some manner.

Throughout *Operations Due Diligence* I avoid identifying specific department structures, but I haven't been able to avoid it completely. I occasionally refer to a specific department in order to make a point. There are some traditional organizational structures that are used by many businesses, but other structures may also be valid. If I assumed a specific organizational structure, readers might infer that one structure was better than another. That implication was clearly not my intent, and readers wouldn't be entering a due diligence with the correct focus if they had a preconceived organizational structure in mind.

An alternate way to look at an organization is to examine the *transaction points* that occur between each of the operations infrastructures and each of the functional groups of the business (see Figure 3.2). In this view, you would be assessing the way the work flows as tasks progress through the business. Assessing the format of each transaction point (forms, databases, work product hand-offs, and so on) will help you to better understand the control structure of the business. Do product managers, for instance, have the authority to give product direction and make product-related decisions across the organization? Many businesses use cross-functional teams to find common solutions that span each of the infrastructure areas, allowing the business to optimize the infrastructure and make the operations more efficient.

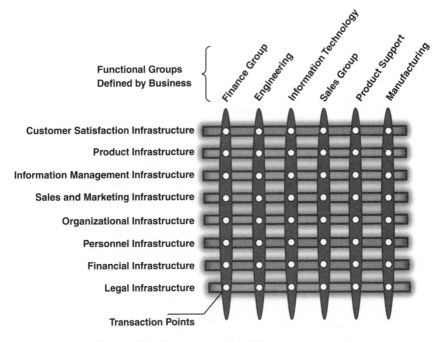

Figure 3.2 Cross-Functional Transaction Points

Assessing an organization by looking at its cross-functional transaction points will give you an operations view of the business and create a tool for further exploration. Looking at the data format at each of the transaction points, for instance, will tell you whether the business does things consistently across its operations. If multiple data formats are used at each point, you may have identified an operations risk. This view also provides direct targets within the business for potential operations research to further improve its efficiency in the future.

PART TWO

Exploring in Depth

"A thing is not proved just because no one has ever questioned it."

—*Denis Diderot (1713–1784)*

CHAPTER 4

Assessment of the Customer Satisfaction Infrastructure

In 1849 the discovery of gold in California caused thousands of men to move from the farms and cities of the east to take up the rugged life of gold miners in the west. As they roamed the hills and streams of California, they were usually dirty, wet, and exposed to the natural elements. The clothes they wore had to be able to survive these conditions, often for an extended period of time. The blue jeans worn by sailors at the time met most of the miners' requirements. The sailors' jeans were rugged and made for extended exposure to the elements. Sailors, however, didn't have to climb mountains, move rocks, and perform many of the other jobs the miners faced. The denim material the jeans were made of was tough, but the miners weren't satisfied with them because they had to constantly patch and repair their jeans, which were literally being pulled apart at the seams.

Jacob Davis was a tailor in California whose business grew by making jeans for the miners. He bought the denim for his jeans from a San Francisco cloth merchant named Levi Strauss. But even though Davis was using high-quality denim, he continued to hear complaints about the jeans from the miners. So he searched for a way to improve the design to better meet the miners' needs for more rugged clothing. He solved the problem by using copper rivets to reinforce the jeans at the points where they became strained, and he was eventually able to produce jeans that satisfied the miners' needs. Davis then approached Strauss to see if he would invest in Davis's new design, and Strauss made the investment. They went into business together to mass produce the new jeans, eventually filing a patent for the new design. Because of their history of customer satisfaction, Levi jeans remain a leading product today.

The entire experience a customer has with a business, with its products and its representatives, needs to be managed through the customer satisfaction infrastructure. Satisfied customers become repeat customers; they tell their friends and remain loyal to a business they feel has given them value. And yet businesses often underestimate how important customer satisfaction is to their success. A surprisingly high number of businesses fail to incorporate customer satisfaction into their business in the form of a system that is integrated and managed with the rest of their operations.

Some businesses do recognize the importance of achieving high levels of customer satisfaction, but they manage it like an artificial facade over the front door rather than integrating customer satisfaction into the business from the foundation up. These businesses openly advertise that their goal is customer satisfaction, but they take few steps to ensure that customer satisfaction has actually been implemented throughout their continuing operations. These businesses handle customer satisfaction organically, in an ad hoc manner, dealing with each situation as it arises, but never proactively managing customer satisfaction with the goal of increasing sales. If a business depends on recurring sales, nothing could present greater risk or greater opportunity than satisfying its customers. *How does the business manage customer satisfaction?*

Satisfaction guaranteed! It's as common to hear this slogan in advertising as it is to hear Amen in church. Why is this offer made for so many products in so many industries?

Customer satisfaction is mostly an emotional state, which makes it difficult to measure. Nevertheless, all businesses need to establish a plan for managing customer satisfaction on a continuous basis. *Does the business measure its level of customer satisfaction periodically?*

Many of the methods used for managing customer satisfaction start with the use of surveys or customer focus sessions. Customer satisfaction surveys have to be implemented with care though. Customers don't like to take the time to complete surveys, and, even when incentives are offered, they often don't fill them out accurately. The most accurate measure of customer satisfaction of course is recurring product sales, but waiting for sales results is risky, and it indicates that the sales strategy is being adjusted by trial and error. After product sales fall off, the reputation of the business has already been established, and it may be too late to make changes. *Does the business plan rely on high levels of customer satisfaction to drive recurring sales?*

Many businesses publish customer satisfaction guidelines that instruct employees how to interact with customers. These guidelines include logging and tracking all customer interactions, comments, commitments, and complaints; maintaining customer confidentiality; dealing with rude customers; tracking customer response times; and any other guidelines specific to the business or market. *Does the business publish customer satisfaction guidelines defining how employees will interact with customers?*

When asked, "Who manages customer satisfaction?" the answer most often received will be, "Everyone. All employees are responsible for customer satisfaction." This is correct, however, because one way to find out if the business is managing its level of customer satisfaction is to ask, "Who is responsible for directing this function?" Like all critical business functions, someone should be identified with the specific responsibility for managing customer satisfaction. *Who is responsible for managing customer satisfaction?*

CUSTOMER SATISFACTION AS A COMPETITIVE DISCRIMINATOR

Customer satisfaction is often the result of the customers' experience with one particular product, and this experience then establishes the customers' perception of the entire business. However, the customers' perception of the product and business is also a result of what they hear about a product rather than their direct experience using it. "I heard that product is expensive" or "My neighbor has one, and it's always in the shop getting fixed" or "It's just too hard to learn to use that software." Of course, interactions with those customers who have had direct experience with a product can be a business's opportunity to drive customer satisfaction and improve recurring sales. "I bought one of the company's products before, and the way the company stood behind it was great." A business can manage its customer satisfaction by creating a market image that drives its customer satisfaction reputation. The business can establish its reputation as a discount house or as a high-end provider of quality products. *Is customer satisfaction a competitive discriminator for the business?*

Figure 4.1 Competitive Discriminators

The reputation of a business is often tied to one of three factors: cost, reliability, or usability (see Figure 4.1). For instance, Toyotas were more expensive than Chevys as long as they were perceived to be more reliable. When Toyota ran into problems with sudden acceleration in the company's vehicles, its prices dropped quickly. Toyota had to work hard and advertise extensively to restore its previously untarnished reputation for quality. The cost, reliability, and usability of a product are the drivers of customer satisfaction.

Cost, reliability, and usability are competitive discriminators that customers continuously use to compare a product against the competition. Sometimes this comparison will be made as a very formal assessment, and other times it will be a subconscious comparison based solely on the customers' perceptions of the products. *Which of the three customer satisfaction discriminators (cost, reliability, and usability) does the business have a reputation for leading in?*

Cost

Customers look at the full life cycle cost of using a product, not just its price. The perceived cost of a product includes the customers' full life cycle expense when using the product. This includes the purchase price of the product plus any other expenses associated with the product's use, such as maintenance, training and labor costs, the cost of the computers that a software product runs on, and any other expenses needed to make the product operational. The value that customers associate with a product is the difference between the life cycle cost of the product and the savings they realize from its use. Even if customers never actually calculate these numbers, they will hold a perception of the value of the product. Boy did I get a great deal!

The miners Jacob Davis sold to may have felt that the price they paid for the sailors' jeans they originally used was fair, but the life cycle cost for the jeans probably seemed high if they considered the time they spent repairing them instead of panning for gold. Even if the Levi jeans cost a little more, they allowed the miners to spend more time working so, in their eyes, the Levi jeans offered greater value.

Customers use products because the products provide utility or because the products save them time or make them money. If a product is discounted or priced low, customers may perceive the low price as an indicator of low quality. If a competitive product includes the cost of a maintenance contract in its price or requires less training, then the life cycle cost of the competitive product will appear lower, even if the purchase price is higher. The product may cost less, but if it's so complex to use that it takes a highly skilled employee to operate it, than the customer perception will be that it is an expensive product.

Whether they do it formally or informally, customers will keep a mental balance sheet for using the product, and they will compare the perceived value of one product against another. *What are the customers' perceived life cycle cost and return on investment (ROI) for the use of the business's products?*

Reliability

Jacob Davis's original jeans had to be repaired constantly so the miners complained about the lack of reliability of the jeans. Improving their reliability meant increasing their value to the miners. The customers' perception of product reliability often goes beyond the product itself. Their perception of product reliability comes from their experience when buying the product (or "what my neighbor said about it when she bought one"), and it includes their perception of all the *customer facing operations* of the business (the points where customers interact with the business in any manner). For instance, support functions like product maintenance are also seen as elements of the product's reliability when the business operates a call center.

Customers expect the product to work or they wouldn't buy it. But they also need to believe that the business and the people they deal with are reliable. "I couldn't get a live person on the phone when I needed help with the installation."

The perceived reliability of a product is also determined by the way the business responds when customers have a problem. Does the business seem stable, and will it be there for its customers in the future if they need it? Reliability extends to all functions of the business. Customers want to be able to establish a rapport with their sales representatives and other employees of the business. They need to feel they are being treated fairly by the billing department. They need to feel they are able to influence the future direction of R&D to meet their growing needs. And they need to be able to speak with management if they have a problem. Customers want the business to be a reliable resource. The timeliness of product deliveries is another area in which customer satisfaction is driven by the reliability of a business. Delivering products and product upgrades to customers at the time they are promised tells the customers that they can rely on the business to support their own schedules and helps strengthen the business's rapport with its own customers. *Has the business established a reputation for reliability with its customers?*

Usability

The usability of a product includes all of the product's features and their ease of use, how well the product's functionality matches the customer's needs and expectations, and how well the product matches the user's skill level. In an attempt to make products more competitive, businesses often overdesign products, adding so many features that the product becomes far more complex than the customer can practically use. This problem is common with products developed for use across a broad market. "Look, this phone is better because it comes with a camera and GPS built in." "Yes, but I don't know how to use a GPS, and I don't need a camera so why should I pay for it?" "Because they are standard in this model!"

Products that require a higher level of operator skill than the average user has will quickly frustrate the user. This is particularly true for commercial products targeted to businesses whose employees' skills are below those required to use the products. Alternately, products that fall below the customers' skill level risk being passed by for products that offer greater functionality. Determining the correct level of usability is difficult, but mismatching the usability of a product with the users' skills can represent a significant risk.

Jacob Davis recognized that denim jeans met most of the miners' requirements but not all of them. He improved the jeans by reinforcing the denim rather than switching to another material such as leather that would exceed their needs and be more expensive than denim. *What method does the business use to match the usability of its products to the skill levels of its customers?*

CUSTOMER SATISFACTION METRICS

Customer satisfaction metrics need to be tracked throughout product development, beginning with the definition of the requirements and continuing through design, implementation, and testing. Each product design change must consider the impact the change will have on the eventual cost, usability, and reliability of the product. *Does the business identify and collect customer satisfaction metrics throughout the life cycle of the product?*

Employees need to be asked to make a personal commitment to achieving high levels of customer satisfaction, and they need to understand the impact their job has on the customers' experience with the business. One way to accomplish this is for customer satisfaction metrics to be fed back as an element of each employee's performance appraisal. "You are rude to customers" or "You go out of your way to help customers" provides important feedback that reemphasizes the customer satisfaction goals of the business. However, this type of statement alone is very subjective. Metrics-based statements such as "Fifty percent of the assemblies you made failed final inspection" provide a much stronger message. *Does the business train its employees about the importance of customer satisfaction?*

Customers hope they never have to contact product support, but most people understand that products do break and things can go wrong.

When this happens, the support the customers receive must be professional, thorough, and effective. The way the business responds to customer problems can be turned into a real opportunity to change a bad experience into a positive one. Metrics such as response time provide tools to help manage customer satisfaction. *Does the business measure product support response time as an element of customer satisfaction?*

Similarly, customers would rather not have to go through extensive training to use a product, but if they do need product training, the training needs to be thorough and effective.

The more complex a product is, the more customers will have to rely on product support and training services, and these must be provided to the highest standards. *Does the business offer product support and product training that are compatible with the complexity of the product?*

HUMAN FACTORS ENGINEERING

The role of human factors engineering is to match the usability of a product to the skill level of its intended users. Unfortunately, human factors engineering is another area where many businesses try to cut corners by leaving the design of the user interfaces in the hands of their design engineering staff, which often has had no formal human factors training. *Does the business employ human factors engineering as a discipline in its development process, or is human factors engineering treated as an ad hoc method?*

The engineering staff become too close to the product to recognize that the functionality they are adding may appear as needless complexity or even silliness to the end user. "Why did they bury the fuse box so far under the dashboard of my car that I have to lie on my back on the floor to reach it?" Or, "Why isn't that function on my computer screen when I need it?" The result is that products that should be easy to use can quickly frustrate the user.

Consider all the jokes you've heard about DVD players on which the clock is never set and continues to blink 12:00 because the user couldn't figure out how to set the correct time. The people who designed the DVD player probably put a lot of thought into the operation of the DVD, but the clock function was treated as an afterthought, and its usability wasn't considered important to the basic function of the device. A function as simple as setting a clock suddenly becomes overly complex and represents a source of irritation for the customer. On the other hand, there are some complex products that seem easy to use. Think about the last car you rented. Did you need any special instructions to operate it, or did you just turn the key and drive away? Of course, years before you had to learn the rules of the road and the basic operations of an automobile, but product standardization like the positioning of the controls in automobiles frequently includes human factors engineering, and product designers must be aware of these standards. Imagine the results if you rented a car and found the gas pedal and the brake pedal were reversed. *Does human factors engineering drive the design of products?*

The level of customer satisfaction is highly affected by the customers' level of frustration when they begin using a product. Some products are complex by their nature. Even in these cases, an attempt should be made to lower the product complexity, such as through automation of complex functions.

Early entry products are notorious for being overly complex. Over time, as competitors find easier ways to add similar functionality, the original product starts to be seen as difficult to use. Human factors engineering offers an opportunity to overcome customer frustration with a product, and it should be incorporated as a design element of the customer satisfaction infrastructure when product complexity is an identified risk.

Human factors engineering also offers a potential opportunity for capturing patentable intellectual property when designing breakthrough products because these products are able to establish the standards before others enter the market. Of course, if there are established product standards and the business has not complied with these standards, it has taken a big risk and needs to be able to explain the rationale behind its decision. *Has the business complied with established standards in the design of its products?*

Product development risks can be mitigated by reviewing the user interface with the customer early in the product development process. If customers are asked to participate in the definition of a product's user interface in advance, you will mitigate the risk of the customers' changing their mind mid-development. This also helps provide focus for the development team on the end goal. By defining the user interfaces early, you have the opportunity to control the scope of its design effort. *Does the product development process include an early design of the user interfaces?*

PRODUCT SPECIFICATIONS

Product development starts with the definition of a requirements baseline captured in the specification. This baseline is then used to drive the product design, build, and test processes. Figure 4.2 depicts a simple product development process (also referred to as a *waterfall*).

The specification is the foundation for all development activities. The more stable the foundation, the more efficiently the development will be completed. For the product to be successful, the specification must reflect the customers' needs as closely as possible.

The closer the product aligns with the customers' needs, the higher the level of customer satisfaction that will be attained. The first step in developing a new product is to perform a requirements analysis that establishes a baseline of the customers' needs that the product must fulfill. The requirements baseline is then documented in a specification that is used to drive the product's design. *Does the business have a defined process for analyzing and prioritizing customers' needs into a requirements baseline?*

The specification forms a baseline that defines all the product features including all of the product's functional, physical, and performance characteristics. The requirements baseline has to be managed in order to establish a cost and schedule budget for development projects. If the baseline isn't managed, then a significant cost or schedule risk (or both) will exist. When the product baseline is allowed to float (referred to as *requirements*

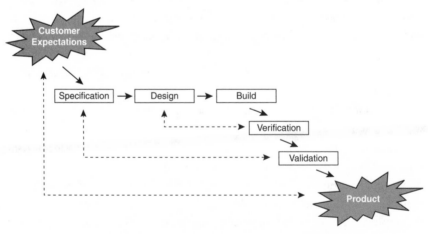

Figure 4.2 The Product Development Process

creep), the development team members aren't focused because they do not have a shared vision of the end product and they may not be able to reach agreement on the end goal of the development. *Does the business manage the requirements baseline for developmental products?*

Products that offer more features are not necessarily more competitive. By adding extra features, the design team may have added cost and complexity that the customers don't want or need. Products that closely match the customers' needs will be more competitive. The product specification is the place where we define the baseline of requirements that product development will include for each release of the product. Overspecifying a product (that is, adding more features than the customers need or want to pay for) can result in a significant customer satisfaction risk as much as underspecifying the product can (that is, not including all of the features customers need).

Products that are underspecified may not be usable or salable. Products that are overspecified include features that are expensive to develop and add needless cost and complexity that go beyond what the customers may be willing to pay or that exceed the customers' skill level. Overspecifying a product also increases the risk that the product will be harder to maintain or will be delivered late to the market. "Our product release was late because we decided we could add a GPS to the cell phone." "But I didn't need the GPS, and I bought someone else's phone because I just couldn't wait any longer for yours." *Who is responsible for prioritizing which product requirements will make it into production?*

Development teams occasionally find themselves in situations in which managers or sales representatives continually ask for the addition of just one more item, which they now believe is absolutely critical (but had not previously thought of). The result is that the development cost and schedule continue to creep. There needs to be a process in place to establish interim goals and milestones that the development team members can work toward to allow them to efficiently move the product from concept to completion. Someone needs to be assigned the authority for managing this process, including making decisions regarding the cost and schedule scope of the project. The person (or group) that controls this process becomes the product release authority that determines when the product has been completed to a level where it can be released to the market. *Who manages the requirements baseline, and is this person the product release authority?*

A *change control board* (CCB) with stakeholders from across the various functional groups is often given responsibility for controlling changes to the requirements baseline. The board's role is to prioritize any changes that would impact the cost and schedule for a product's development. Having an active CCB will help mitigate developmental cost and schedule risks by prioritizing the requirements that must be included or that can be delayed until a future release.

Following an investment, you will also be a stakeholder, and you may want to consider at what point you will either become a member of the CCB or start monitoring the actions of the CCB in order to mitigate investment risk and identify opportunities to help set the strategic direction of the product. *Does the business operate a cross-functional change control board?*

EVOLUTIONARY DEVELOPMENT

There are cases, particularly with the development of breakthrough products, in which the full scope of a product, or components of the product, cannot be fully understood at the outset of development. In these situations, the development team may need to proceed into design with only a conceptual understanding of the full scope of the end product. The design of the final product must evolve as more knowledge is gained through the design process. Evolutionary development is commonly used for the creation of breakthrough hardware and software products because it defers the questions about the product that reasonably may be answered only after completing some initial level of design.

An automobile manufacturer, for example, may be able to specify whether a new model will need a six- or eight-cylinder engine without much trouble. The business knows the capability of these engines. If it is developing a new model that includes breakthrough technology, such as integrating a revolutionary new hydrogen engine, the development team members may have to complete the design to the point where they know the new model's approximate weight before designing a new engine to power it. Since the team members' design is iterative and they start without knowing all of the design parameters, they need to design the new engine to meet the performance parameters of the car. They must start the development with both schedule and cost risks that must eventually be mitigated.

Because evolutionary development allows part of the requirements baseline to remain incomplete, the risk must be aggressively managed. "Agile development" is an evolutionary development method used to mitigate risk in these situations. With Agile development, risk is managed by exposing critical components early and carefully controlling the scope of their development. *Is the business using evolutionary development methods such as Agile development?*

Paul McMahon is one of the leading experts on Agile software development. McMahon describes Agile development as follows:

> With Agile approaches we don't do all the requirements work up front. We continue to collaborate to ensure we are getting the best value for the customer throughout the project. However, we need to have a way to bound the work, if we are to manage it to a fixed schedule. This is the intent of the Scope document. The Scope document provides a reference for collaboration. For a Scope document to be effective, it must also be used by everyone who is collaborating. This includes both customers and development personnel.
>
> On both Agile and traditional projects, one of the most difficult tasks is eliciting the real needs and expectations of customers and getting them agreed to by major stakeholders. By building a Scope document and actively engaging the key stakeholders early in a review and approval cycle, a basis for project success is established. (*Source*: Paul McMahon, *Integrating CMMI and Agile Development*, © Pearson Education, Boston, 2010.)

When applied correctly, Agile development is used to control the scope of the development, and risk is actively prioritized and mitigated.

The term *Agile* is often misapplied. When misapplied, it can mean that product development is open ended due to insufficient requirements analysis or design and that the scope of the project cannot be determined or controlled. The development is not being managed. If you are assessing a business that claims to be using Agile development, proceed with caution. This is a good place to check the BS Quotient. What you may be hearing is: "We don't know what our schedule or cost is so we're calling it an Agile development, but we're not rigorously following an Agile method to mitigate our risks." *If Agile development is being used, how is the scope of the project being managed?*

> Evolutionary development tries to balance research opportunity against development risk.

Evolutionary development is used when there is a need to balance research opportunity against development risk. If the business is using evolutionary development, you are accepting early development risk against the opportunity of participating in the development of a breakthrough product. In order to understand your risk, your assessment must determine whether the development team is truly following an Agile method or just paying it lip service. *Has the specification of the product evolved sufficiently to determine which requirements will be included in the production version, how long it will take to get to market, and what resources will be required to get the product into production?*

PRODUCT TESTING

During the early twentieth century, Bell Labs installed the first large-scale telephone systems. At that time, the mass production of electronic components, particularly components that had to function outside in the elements, was largely an unknown, untested science. Since telephone systems relied on components that were installed in hard-to-reach places, like on top of telephone poles and buried underground, fully exposed to the weather, the ability to manufacture uniform products that worked reliably in the elements was critical to Bell Labs' success. Replacing failed components is expensive after they have been installed in the field, and the reliability of the entire system could be impacted by the failure of a single component.

Walter A. Shewhart was an engineer working for Bell Labs in 1924, and he was given responsibility for improving the reliability of the system. Shewhart recognized that it was impossible to test every single component used in the system, and so in response he wrote the first paper on the use of statistical sampling for quality control. In his analysis Shewhart tied the quality of a product back to the process used to manufacture it, and he showed that product variations could be controlled by continuously improving the manufacturing process. By linking the cause of a failure to the manufacturing process (Shewhart called it "assignable cause") as opposed to random failures (or "chance cause"), if the process could be brought into statistical control, it could be relied on to consistently produce quality components.

In his writings Shewhart drew a simple diagram to help describe the statistical distribution of component failures. This diagram became known as the "bell curve" (see Figure 4.3). While most people today are accustomed to seeing a bell curve used for tracking the distribution of student test scores, the bell curve continues to apply to the statistical tracking of product reliability in the same way it was originally used. It shows the distribution of product test scores. By continually identifying the association of high failure distribution back to the development process, the process can be improved, resulting in higher-quality products. Product testing is a statistical measure of how well a product performs according to the customers' expectations, and it is measured by how closely the product complies with its defined requirements. *Does the business track statistical test samples to the development process?*

The perceived quality of a product is a measure of how well the product meets the customers' expectations. When customers buy a product and it doesn't perform as they anticipated, they quickly become dissatisfied with it, even though the product might work as designed and technically has not failed. "My new car runs fine, but it just doesn't have the pickup the salesman said it would." When a product fails to perform as the customers expect, the customers' perception is that its quality is low and therefore so is their resulting level of customer satisfaction, even though the product is not actually broken. Customer satisfaction is maximized when the defined requirements for the product closely align with the customers' expectations.

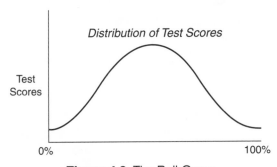

Figure 4.3 The Bell Curve

The customer satisfaction infrastructure provides the framework that links customer expectations, requirement analysis, product verification, and quality assurance together. If this linkage is not made, then there is a tremendous risk that the business will gain a reputation for low-quality products. *Does the business track product requirements to product testing and quality assurance?*

To ensure closure between customer expectations and product performance, testing needs to be performed at two levels.

The first level of testing is *verification testing*. Verification testing assures the "as-built" quality of the product, meaning that the product works as engineering designed it (it hasn't broken). This testing is usually performed as a development activity.

The second level of testing is *validation testing*. Validation testing ensures that the product is performing as the customers intended it. If a product fails during validation testing, it is either because the requirements analysis or the design was performed incorrectly. Requirements were missed, or invalid requirements were included in the specification. Validation testing ensures that the product meets all of its specified requirements. *Does the business perform customer acceptance and validation testing?*

Remember, the product may work as designed but still fail to meet the customers' expectations if the requirements analysis was not performed accurately. Verification tests are performed for both developmental and production products. *Does the business perform verification testing for both developmental and production products?*

Testing is a costly activity and can quickly become the critical path on product release schedules. Your goal when assessing how well verification and validation testing have been performed is to determine whether the business has done sufficient product testing to assure the quality of the product. One way to accomplish this is to look at the product test logs to understand how many issues have been identified and closed and how many remain open. *Does the business maintain product test logs that list open and closed test issues?*

Investors occasionally attempt to minimize their risk by stating that they will commit funds only if the product has completed testing and has already been released. There is a risk with this strategy. Simply requiring the business to release the product prior to receiving an investment can have a negative effect because it creates an incentive for the business to cut corners. The investors assume a risk by volunteering to take themselves out of the verification loop because they miss the hands-on opportunity to witness the performance of the product. If this is a strategic investment and you are planning to proceed in any case, you might want to become involved early to ensure that sufficient testing is performed. Cutting corners on product testing becomes an attractive alternative for businesses that need to get their widget on the market as a term of completing an acquisition or investment deal. Changing the status of a product from developmental to production—"Put it out now and we can fix it later"—is very risky, but it frequently happens. This becomes a great risk for investors who haven't fully assessed the quality of the product. *Was the product released to the market too soon?*

If the product is released to the market before all of its latent bugs have been fixed and it is deployed to the field too soon, then the cost for repairs becomes far greater than they would have been if they had been resolved prior to shipping. When products fail in the field, it means incurring additional costs to return the product or the cost to send staff into the field to make repairs. There is also a risk that this will impact the customers' operations, which will lower customer satisfaction even further.

> If the product fails after it is shipped, the cost to make field repairs may not be the only concern!

If the product fails after it is shipped, than the cost to make field repairs may not be the only concern. There may also be legal liability for products that are shipped, particularly if they have known problems, not to mention the damage that is done to the reputation of the business. This liability could be criminal as well as civil. Of course, limitations of liability for the investors can be addressed as a term in all investment agreements, but this doesn't eliminate the potential risk of loss of future business due to product problems. *Do any previously shipped products have known problems for which the business may be liable?*

Hardware materials degrade, consumable components become spent, and the environments in which hardware must work are highly variable. Customers expect a product to work, and they want it to work for a long time.

Hardware products must work reliably in their intended environments. The environment in which hardware must work could include working in the home, in a car, on a boat, in outer space, or in inner space (such as a pacemaker). The environmental requirements for hardware products should include a definition of the environmental reliability standards the product must meet. The standards that were used to make the clock radio on your nightstand are far different from those used to make a pacemaker. Hardware verification tests should be designed to ensure that the product complies with these standards. *Does the business define the environmental requirements for hardware products?*

You probably wouldn't buy a pacemaker made to the same standards as a clock radio, but would you be willing to pay the price for a clock radio that was made to the same standards as a pacemaker? Probably not! Hardware reliability is a function of production costs. Mission critical devices such as pacemakers and satellites need to be tested to ensure that they continue to work in their anticipated environments. And all products need to be tested to ensure that they work reliably through their anticipated life cycle. *Are products' life cycles tested to ensure that they meet their reliability standards?*

Even products as simple as clock radios must be manufactured according to commercial standards such as the Underwriters Laboratories (UL) standards. UL certification means that the reliability of a product has been tested and verified by an independent third party. *Have commercial products been certified to UL standards?*

Aligning the reliability of a product with the criticality of its mission is a key driver in determining the product's eventual price. The mission of a clock radio and the mission of a pacemaker are quite different because the pacemaker has to be made to much higher reliability standards. *Do the requirements for hardware products include definitions of the reliability standards the product must meet?*

We expect to pay more for highly reliable products than we pay for non–mission critical commercial products like an alarm clock. In addition, the level of the product's liability can also be driven directly by how mission critical the hardware is. *How mission critical is the reliability of the hardware product?*

Hardware testing is performed at the component, assembly, and end item levels. Tests need to be conducted according to a well-thought-out test strategy that is documented in a test plan. Product destruction tests are often conducted for mission critical products to validate their performance at the extremes of their operating ranges. Stress tests are often environment simulations where the product is able to be brought to its extremes artificially. This type of testing can include shock, temperature, and vibration, and it can even extend to testing for specialized environments such as salt spray (for marine products). This type of testing can be expensive and must be carefully planned. The cost of test units to be destroyed during tests should be budgeted items. *Is there a documented test strategy, and is there evidence of the testing that has been conducted to date?*

As part of the original goal to land a person on the moon, the National Aeronautics and Space Administration (NASA) established a strenuous testing program to ensure the safety of the crews. Testing was extensive because this was clearly a mission critical operation. The *Apollo 11* mission was the first manned mission to land on the moon. On July 20, 1969, the lunar module *Eagle* carrying Neil A. Armstrong and Edwin E. Aldrin separated from the command module piloted by Michael Collins. The *Eagle* dropped out of lunar orbit and headed toward the Sea of Tranquility. After separating from the command module, the rendezvous radar on the lunar module, which was used for guiding close operations between the two spacecraft, was accidentally left on, and it continued to provide data to the computer on the lunar module during its descent.

As the landing began, the *Eagle*'s navigation and guidance computer reported several unusual "program alarms" as it guided the descent. The lunar module was reported 4 seconds further along its planned trajectory than had been anticipated, and the *Eagle* was going to overshoot its planned landing site. As the *Eagle* approached the surface of the moon, it became apparent to Neil Armstrong that the computer was guiding them toward a large crater. Armstrong took manual control of the lunar module, overriding the computer, and he guided it to a landing with about 30 seconds of fuel remaining. The system design had not anticipated an event in which the radar would be left on during landing. It was supposed to be turned off during the landing phase.

Not all software bugs are code bugs. Software also fails because its design was flawed. In the case of the lunar module, the developers failed to consider all of the possible scenarios that might be encountered, and as a result of this design flaw, unanticipated results were returned. By today's standards, the computers on the lunar module were unsophisticated, and the software programs were not very complex. The program alarms were indications that the computer wasn't completing all of its processing tasks. The computer was spending unplanned time processing the extra data coming from the rendezvous radar that had continued to run during descent. The programmers hadn't anticipated the possibility of extra data coming from a system that was supposed to be turned off, and as a result they hadn't tested for that scenario. The quick actions and daring of the crew saved the mission from being aborted or ending in a great catastrophe. The software had been tested to ensure that it worked as designed, but the design hadn't been tested for this contingency.

Software, like hardware, can be mission critical, and this can have an effect on customer satisfaction and product reliability. To overcome this problem and ensure that all of the scenarios in which the software will be used are considered, *software use cases* are defined as part of the product requirements analysis. The more complex the product, the more time the design team will need for developing and documenting the potential use-case scenarios. *Are software use-case scenarios documented?*

Unlike hardware, software doesn't break down or wear out. Or does it?

Unlike hardware, software doesn't break down or wear out. Or does it? Of course not! But software does fail. Software fails whenever it produces an unexpected result. As software gets more complex, the number of potential paths or combinations of paths through the code continues to increase. As the complexity of the software grows, it quickly becomes unrealistic or impossible to test for all of the potential combinations of variables and paths through the code that could eventually occur and cause a failure. The failure doesn't occur because the software has worn out as with hardware but because the user eventually executed a code path that had a latent error in it and the result returned by the software wasn't the anticipated result. And this is the major difference between hardware and software. Over time, hardware wears out and its failure rate increases. Over time, software doesn't wear out, and once you've executed a path successfully and it has worked, it will continue to work. Over time, the failure rate of software goes down. *Are complexity metrics collected to determine the reliability of software products?*

The longer software runs, the greater the likelihood it will have traversed all of the possible paths and any latent bugs will have been found. Software becomes more reliable over time while hardware becomes less reliable. Software testing is a statistical problem. It requires careful thought and planning to implement a test strategy that optimizes the odds of discovering problems within the allotted budget and schedule constraints. *Is there a documented test plan?*

The use of automated software test tools helps to overcome the statistical test requirements for complex software products, but while the use of these tools to automate the process is often necessary, they come with a cost. The care and feeding of automated software test tools requires the development of an effective test strategy (based on the use of the tool), the design of detailed test cases, and the population and continuing maintenance of these cases to support recurring product tests. All of which must be budgeted as part of the test plan. *Does the business use and budget the cost of automated test tools?*

Over time the *mean time between failures* (MTBF) for hardware decreases and failures accelerate as the hardware components start to reach the limits of their useful life. The MTBF for software increases over time (but is never assumed to get to zero) because over time the likelihood of running into a code path that has not been executed goes down.

There is nothing magical about software testing even if it does occasionally seem to be practiced by wizards who have been schooled in the black arts. Software testing requires an ability to comprehend the interactions of multilayered architectures and to anticipate how the code will interact within its software environment. Correctly testing software of even moderate complexity requires a strong understanding of statistics, including a good grasp of probability theory.

Some schools of thought will tell you that even moderately complex software is in fact not testable. The reality is that you cannot reasonably guarantee that a software product is 100 percent free of bugs in all of the possible configurations that it may encounter during use. The time it would take to test all of the possible combinations is well beyond any practical limit, including the useful life of the program or the programmer. The question then becomes: If you can't fully test the software, is there an acceptable number of bugs with which the product can be released to the market? The answer is that it depends on the criticality of the application. And this answer is rarely understood or accepted by the users of the software. Customers will see absolutely no reason why any software product hasn't been tested to perfection. *How many customer installations has the software had, and how many estimated run-time hours does it have?*

Customers understand that hardware will break, wear out, or fail in some manner over time. We plan to deal with repairs when the problems occur. We would all love to have a car that could last for 10 or 15 years without some form of breakdown, but we also know what a car that reliable would cost, and instead, we accept a warranty that will cover the cost of the repair when one is needed. Software will also fail over time, but the more use it has, the more reliable it will become. *Is the product a "first release," or is it an upgrade to a previously shipped product (and therefore it has been tested through wide customer use)?*

PRODUCT SUPPORT

Of course, no matter how much effort a business puts into building user-friendly, reliable, high-quality products, it is inevitable that some customers may still run into problems. And when they do have a problem, it's the way the business responds to the problem that customers will remember. If the business is proactive in giving its support, the customers will be left with a favorable impression. Their experience will determine whether they will purchase from the business again.

Furthermore, when product problems occur, the business has an opportunity to cement its future relationships with its customers and turn these events into positive encounters. *Does the business offer long-term maintenance support for its products?*

Product support can provide an additional revenue opportunity for some businesses that operate their product support group as a profit center. The advantages of operating product support as a profit center is that the cost for maintenance of fielded products is more readily tracked, and maintenance revenues can be used to support increased product testing. This is particularly important if the business tracks its cost-of-quality metrics. *Is the product support group operated as a profit center?*

Supporting products after they have been shipped becomes an important element of the customer satisfaction infrastructure. Businesses offer a wide range of product support services, and it's important to understand exactly which of these services are provided by the business and why. The Product Support Services sidebar lists many of the product support services businesses commonly offer.

Product Support Services

Maintenance agreements   Customer advocates
Telephone support   Customer satisfaction surveys
E-mail support   Remote log-in
Online user forums and blogs   Automated upgrade notices
24/7 support   In-house training
On-site support   On-site training

Maintenance agreements are another way to offer customers additional value. By offering maintenance agreements that include extended functions such as remote product monitoring, product upgrades, technical publications, and online user forums and blogs, customers are being brought closer, and they become champions of the product.

Remember, maintenance agreements generally start after the product warrantee ends. Some of the maintenance services may not be included in the warrantee, and they can be added as "up sells" or as additional features if included in the initial product price. Including "complimentary" features initially can be a good way to expose customers to these benefits that you will ask them to purchase later. *Does the business offer maintenance agreements on a fee-for-service basis?*

Telephone support offers the customer direct access to live operators who are qualified to directly and immediately help resolve their problems. For complex products or products that have been shipped to the field with a high level of problems, this type of support can generate high customer satisfaction. Retaining a trained staff to handle these calls can be costly. This cost is driven by the anticipated call volume. There are other potential roles for this type of support staff including those of product testers and customer advocates. *Does the business provide telephone support for its products?*

E-mail support is another way to provide a direct response to customers; however, unlike telephone support, customers must wait (often
days) for the response. The advantage of e-mail support is that it allows
workload to be balanced by the support staff between low and high activity periods, but the disadvantage is that it allows the customers to become
angry while waiting for a response. E-mail responses can be more accurate
than voice mail responses because the support response is not provided
interactively with a live support representative and the representative has
time to research the problem before responding. It may require more itera-
tion to resolve the problem. *Does the business provide e-mail support for
its products?*

Providing 24/7 support is expensive, but it is an absolute requirement
in some industries. There needs to be clear justification for maintaining a
support staff with this type of schedule. One way to look at it is to understand what the working schedule is for the average user of the product.
I worked in the litigation support industry where a court could order evidence to be processed in a very short period of time. Our customers therefore had to be able to work around the clock to meet their court imposed
deadlines, and we were expected to be able to support them at any time as
well. Cost was an issue, which meant that we had to be creative to solve
this requirement. So we paid operators to be "on call" from home and to
work split shifts when a customer notified us of a large trial. *Does the business provide 24/7 support for its products?*

Having a representative be on site to provide customer support is
obviously expensive. Generally, customers can be charged for this type
of support, unless you are sending the field representative in response to
a product problem. Fixing products in the field is expensive. That is why
time and money must be spent testing products prior to shipping them.
Does the business provide on-site support for its products?

Some businesses use their experienced product support staff in other
roles such as in-house customer advocates and product testers. This gives
the product support staff an additional career path beyond answering
the phones in a call center, and it helps the business to better use critical customer satisfaction resources. The product support staff is typically
on the front line with customers, and it is responsible for answering irate
customer phone calls when there is a product problem. This means the
product support staff is much more likely to ensure that the product is bug

free before it's shipped. By splitting shifts between customer support and product testing, the customer support staff is able to bring direct customer feedback into the test and QA process. Because they receive direct customer feedback, the product support staff tends to gain greater insight into the customers' needs making them effective in-house customer advocates. *Does the business provide internal customer advocates for its products?*

Many businesses offer additional or extended value services as part of their maintenance agreements, which provides the businesses with additional recurring maintenance revenue. Expanding the product support services to include functions like conducting customer surveys and feeding this information back into their customer satisfaction metrics can help businesses prioritize their product improvement activities. Other ways in which the product support staff can help businesses improve are monitoring customer call times, analyzing maintenance trends, tracking bug resolutions (how long it takes for problems to be resolved), monitoring training effectiveness (how hard it is for customers to learn how to use the product), and providing feedback on the effectiveness of the product documentation (how helpful the users' guides are to customers). *Does the business provide customer satisfaction surveys for its products? Does the business use customer satisfaction surveys and metrics to target risk areas and prioritize product improvement opportunity areas?*

One way to overcome the isolation customers feel with e-mail support is for the business to sponsor online forums and blogs. Forums and blogs offer customers the opportunity to interact in near real time with a support representative. Responses are delivered in writing, which makes them easier for customers to implement than voice instructions, but it does limit the ability of the representative to interact with customers. An additional tremendous value of online forums and blogs is the ability for customers to interact with one another, often allowing more experienced users to help less experienced users without the use of product support. Becoming part of an online users' forum is a tremendous marketing opportunity. The business must actively manage these services, however. *Does the business provide online user forums and/or blogs for its products?*

With the availability of high-speed Internet connections, software products are now commonly offered with automatic online product upgrade notices and online product downloads. This is an additional opportunity for the business to increase customer value by preempting issues before they are even noticed by the customer. It can also open up additional sales opportunities. *Does the business provide remote support log-in for its software products? Does the business provide automated update notices for its products?*

If the business uses sales channel partners and product resellers, all of the product support functions previously described need to be extended to include support for both the channel partner and for their customers. This may present an opportunity to improve sales by paying special attention to the product support services provided for the channel partners. If the business offers maintenance agreements, then these also represent potential sales for the channel partners and resellers. *Does the business provide product support services for its channel partners and resellers?*

PRODUCT TRAINING

Ideally all products will be so intuitive and easy to use that there will be no need for customer training. In reality, the more complex the product is, the greater the need to offer some form of customer training. Offering fee-based training services provides an additional revenue opportunity for some businesses. *Does the business offer fee-based product training?*

Depending on the type and complexity of the product, customer training can be offered in-house or it can be offered on site at the customer's facility. *Does the business provide in-house training for its products? Does the business provide on-site training for its products?*

Customers will purchase training if the training offers value, such as a shorter learning curve with the product. If the business offers customer training, the training must be well planned and not treated as an afterthought. If training is sold to customers, then all of the product discussions apply to the creation of the training plan. Training becomes a product that needs to be driven by customer requirements, designed, and tested.

Customer feedback should be used to create training requirements, and these requirements should drive the design of the training curricula. Some measure of the training quality (called *training effectiveness*) needs to be established. Training effectiveness can be measured through metrics such as drops in the call volumes being made to the call center after training. *Does the business measure the effectiveness of its customer training products?*

Training courses that are planned and well thought out are great ways to mitigate risk due to product complexity. In addition, they may offer an opportunity to improve customer satisfaction without actually performing an upgrade to the product itself. Customer training sessions also offer a unique opportunity to build a rapport with the customers. This is an ideal opportunity to collect market feedback about what the customers do and do not like about the product, what part of its use they have problems understanding and are growing frustrated with, and so on. Businesses can use these sessions also to gain insight about any additional needs customers may have. *Does the business look at training as an opportunity to collect customer feedback?*

Summary of the Customer Satisfaction Infrastructure Questions

1. How does the business manage customer satisfaction?
2. Does the business measure its level of customer satisfaction periodically?
3. Does the business plan rely on high levels of customer satisfaction to drive recurring sales?
4. Does the business publish customer satisfaction guidelines defining how employees will interact with customers?
5. Who is responsible for managing customer satisfaction?
6. Is customer satisfaction a competitive discriminator for the business?
7. Which of the three customer satisfaction discriminators (cost, reliability, and usability) does the business have a reputation for leading in?
8. What are the customers' perceived life cycle cost and return on investment (ROI) for the use of the business's products?
9. Has the business established a reputation for reliability with its customers?
10. What method does the business use to match the usability of its products to the skill levels of its customers?
11. Does the business identify and collect customer satisfaction metrics throughout the life cycle of the product?
12. Does the business train its employees about the importance of customer satisfaction?

13. Does the business measure product support response time as an element of customer satisfaction?
14. Does the business offer product support and product training that are compatible with the complexity of the product?
15. Does the business employ human factors engineering as a discipline in its development process, or is human factors engineering treated as an ad hoc method?
16. Does human factors engineering drive the design of products?
17. Has the business complied with established standards in the design of its products?
18. Does the product development process include an early design of the user interfaces?
19. Does the business have a defined process for analyzing and prioritizing customers' needs into a requirements baseline?
20. Does the business manage the requirements baseline for developmental products?
21. Who is responsible for prioritizing which product requirements will make it into production?
22. Who manages the requirements baseline, and is this person the product release authority?
23. Does the business operate a cross-functional change control board?
24. Is the business using evolutionary development methods such as Agile development?
25. If Agile development is being used, how is the scope of the project being managed?
26. Has the specification of the product evolved sufficiently to determine which requirements will be included in the production version, how long it will take to get to market, and what resources will be required to get the product into production?
27. Does the business track statistical test samples to the development process?
28. Does the business track product requirements to product testing and quality assurance?
29. Does the business perform customer acceptance and validation testing?

30. Does the business maintain product test logs that list open and closed test issues?
31. Does the business perform verification testing for both developmental and production products?
32. Was the product released to the market too soon?
33. Do any previously shipped products have known problems for which the business may be liable?
34. Does the business define the environmental requirements for hardware products?
35. Are products' life cycles tested to ensure that they meet their reliability standards?
36. Have commercial products been certified to UL standards?
37. Do the requirements for hardware products include definitions of the reliability standards the product must meet?
38. How mission critical is the reliability of the hardware product?
39. Is there a documented test strategy, and is there evidence of the testing that has been conducted to date?
40. Are software use-case scenarios documented?
41. Are complexity metrics collected to determine the reliability of software products?
42. Is there a documented test plan?
43. Does the business use and budget the cost of automated test tools?
44. How many customer installations has the software had, and how many estimated run-time hours does it have?
45. Is the product a "first release," or is it an upgrade to a previously shipped product (and therefore it has been tested through wide customer use)?
46. Does the business offer long-term maintenance support for its products?
47. Is the product support group operated as a profit center?
48. Does the business offer maintenance agreements on a fee-for-service basis?
49. Does the business provide telephone support for its products?
50. Does the business provide e-mail support for its products?
51. Does the business provide 24/7 support for its products?

52. Does the business provide on-site support for its products?
53. Does the business provide internal customer advocates for its products?
54. Does the business provide customer satisfaction surveys for its products?
55. Does the business use customer satisfaction surveys and metrics to target risk areas and prioritize product improvement opportunity areas?
56. Does the business provide online user forums and/or blogs for its products?
57. Does the business provide remote support log-in for its software products?
58. Does the business provide automated update notices for its products?
59. Does the business provide product support services for its channel partners and resellers?
60. Does the business offer fee-based product training?
61. Does the business provide in-house training for its products?
62. Does the business provide on-site training for its products?
63. Does the business measure the effectiveness of its customer training products?
64. Does the business look at training as an opportunity to collect customer feedback?

CHAPTER 5

Assessment of the Production Infrastructure

Thomas Edison had a tremendous idea with the electric light. He expected to use it to light up the world, but he would prove his idea by first lighting up a small part of Manhattan and the small town of Roselle, New Jersey. Edison knew the importance of being first, and he wanted his solution to establish a standard for the industry so he moved quickly to develop and patent his products ahead of his competition. His competition came from George Westinghouse who was also determined to lead the new industry.

Edison believed firmly that the use of direct current (DC) would be the key to power distribution. Westinghouse believed that the use of alternating current (AC) would be better than direct current because it would allow easier, less costly distribution of electricity. And a heated competitive battle quickly began. Each inventor presented a view of his product to the market that supported his own position. Edison, in an attempt to convince the public that alternating current was dangerous, even went to the trouble of building the first electric chair using AC power as a public demonstration of its dangers. In the end, Westinghouse won out, and the world standardized on alternating current. Even though Edison was wrong on this very fundamental issue, the company he founded lasts today because Edison developed an adaptable infrastructure that was able to sustain the future growth of his business.

It's important that investors look beyond the product to gain an understanding of the full potential of a business. All products, even the very best products on the market or the hottest product concepts, can be high-risk investments if the business doesn't have a sufficient production capability and a sound production infrastructure in place to bring the product fully to market. The production infrastructure includes all of the tools, activities, and processes needed to bring a product from concept to mass production. If the production infrastructure of a business is assessed as a weak area, an investment strategy that included updating the production infrastructure could offer a great opportunity for an investor willing to fund the improvement.

When assessing the production infrastructure, remember that you are not only assessing the product or products themselves. You are also assessing the business's ability to produce the products in the planned volumes needed to support the projected revenues. You are assessing the business's ability to deliver the product profitably on a continuing basis into the future.

Since most businesses have more than one product, I use the term *product* rather broadly to indicate the primary product line of the business. The following discussions assume that the business has either a single core product or a suite of products that drives its revenue. You will assess the production infrastructure for each individual product. You will need to determine the scope of your due diligence by deciding whether to assess the production process for a core product of the business or perform an assessment across multiple product lines. This decision is largely determined by the type of business you are assessing and on your investment goals. As a guide, I suggest you conduct your assessment for each product that contributes significantly to the revenue stream of the business. *Is there a product concept, a working prototype, or a working product?*

It takes an investment of capital and a commitment of resources to produce a product. Software development requires computers, tools, and a test environment. Hardware requires machine tools and plastic molds. Even a farm requires tractors to produce its product. Capital invested into the assets that support the production process can allow a business to operate more efficiently and to be more competitive. *Does the business have the capital equipment it needs in place to support production?*

PRODUCT DEVELOPMENT AND PRODUCTION

A good place to begin your exploration of the production infrastructure is by determining how far a product has progressed into the development and production process. You're looking for evidence that products have completed the full development and production cycle. If the products are still in development and haven't moved into production, you need to find out why they haven't. You want to explore what types of problems the business has had while bringing the product to market. Maybe there are technical obstacles to production that indicate potential risks, or maybe the business is experiencing a cash flow problem. These can indicate large potential risks or potential opportunities for investors. If the product is currently in production, the production infrastructure needs to be able to support an expansion to the anticipated larger market volumes that will occur following release. *Is the production capability of the business sufficient to take the product fully to market?*

Products evolve through two distinct phases: development, which is where they are initially designed and created, and production, which is where they are mass produced for the market. As products complete development testing (building on the product test discussion from Chapter 4), they are referred to as "released." Prior to that, products are referred to as "in development." After being released, products are referred to as "in production." The development phase is generally characterized by nonrecurring costs for expenses such as engineering, fixturization, verification testing, and documentation. During production there are generally recurring costs (capital costs such as equipment being the primary exception to this). Developmental products are typically prototypes used for proving the concepts and testing. They are often used as demonstration models shown to potential investors. *Are demonstration products considered prototypes, or are they actual production units?*

If the product is in development and hasn't yet entered into production, how long will it realistically be before the product will enter the market and begin sales? Once this point is determined, it should be possible to accurately estimate what the remaining development costs are likely to be before profits are realized. Bringing a new product to market profitability is always a risky venture. An accurate estimate of time-to-market and cost-to-market helps to mitigate this risk. *Is product development on schedule, and have all technical hurdles been overcome?*

The production and development cost curves shown in Figure 5.1 are typical for evolving hardware products. Determining where developmental products are on this curve is a good way to gain situation awareness about the maturity of the product, and it will help you assess risk or opportunity as a function of life cycle cost. A similar curve for a software product would have higher nonrecurring costs and diminishing production costs. The investment target area would remain the same. *Can the product concept be turned into a salable product **and** make a profit with the planned resources?*

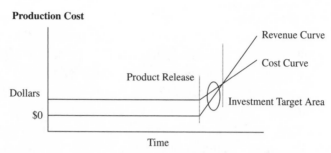

Figure 5.1 The Production and Development Cost Curves

Higher investment risk exists toward the left side of the curve (earlier in development) because neither the product nor the production process has matured or been proven, there is no revenue, and most of the development costs remain. This is the point where a development project has the highest level of nonrecurring development cost. It is also the point where a development project faces the greatest risk of failure. The more mature the product, the lower the investment risk because the product design will have overcome any technical issues, the production infrastructure will have been demonstrated, and the sales revenue can be seen.

The product eventually becomes profitable and self-sufficient. This is also the point where venture capital investors are likely to take over from angel investors. Since the product has attained a cash-positive position, there is a lower risk of failure, and you may not have the same opportunity to buy in. The value of the business will be higher once the product is mature and already on the market and the business has already overcome and mitigated its early production risks. You'll need to have a clear understanding of the maturity of the product when creating your investment strategy. Is your strategy to find good ideas that require development capital such that you are able to "buy in early," or is your strategy to find lower-risk investments where a mature product has already been proven but still has potentially high up-front investment costs? You need to consider this curve carefully when establishing your investment strategy. *How far into the production and development process has the core product progressed?*

The investment target area is the optimal point where the product has been completed and its sales are starting to take off. Because there may be a greater need for funds to support production, marketing, sales, and support, this is the time when the business has the greatest need for financial backing and the opportunity for the investor may be greatest. It's important to be able to properly identify this point. It's the point where the business has released the product but it has not gained enough sales traction for it to become profitable. *Where is the product on the production and development cost curves?*

PRODUCT LIFE CYCLE

The life cycle of a product begins when the product is released (see Figure 5.2). The life cycle has distinct, identifiable phases (inception, sustained sales, obsolescence), and you will need to verify that the position of the product on its life cycle curve aligns with your investment goals. Are you looking for an investment in an innovative new product, for instance? Or are you looking for a more predictable return based on the growth of a well-known and trusted product line? *Where is the product in its life cycle?*

The slope of the product life cycle curve is a risk/opportunity indicator. While Figure 5.2 shows a smooth curve, what we might hope to see is a sharply increasing slope or even a spike when a product is introduced and a slow decline during obsolescence. If the inception curve rises slowly, it may indicate that the product was slow to take off. If the slope of the obsolescence curve indicates a sudden steep drop, it may indicate that the market has turned away from the technology.

When products first enter the market, they go through their inception phase. During this phase, sales (units sold) start to build as the market becomes aware of the product. The marketing plan starts to gain traction, and as customers start to use the new product, they tend to talk about it and share the experience of using it with other potential users, and the number

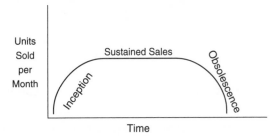

Figure 5.2 The Product Life Cycle Curve

of sales starts to rise. Occasionally demand for a product rises steeply and quickly, and the inception phase can be very short (it might actually look like a spike on the life cycle curve). The business must be able to respond to product demand; if it can't, it risks losing its market. As you perform your assessment, you should be looking at how well the business has managed the inception phase of its products. It's great when there's such high demand for a product that its inception prices are driven up, but if the business meets the demand by cutting corners and the product gets a quick reputation for poor quality, it is not good. *Is the business able to keep product deliveries current with its backlog?*

If the demand for the product was greater than the business was able to produce, why did this happen? Did the business lack the resources to produce the product (a possible opportunity), or was it dependent on critical unavailable product components (a possible risk)? Alternatively, if the business erroneously anticipated a large demand for the product and therefore overproduced it, what went wrong? *Does the business have a large uncommitted inventory that it has not been able to sell?*

Maybe the business created products it was not able to sell because of quality assurance or market problems. As a new product is introduced into the market, the production infrastructure needs to be ready to support that production. Concepts like just-in-time or "Lean Manufacturing" need to be considered both to mitigate cash flow issues and to mitigate production risks. The responses to these questions can be great indicators of production risks and opportunities for investors. *Does the business use Lean Manufacturing techniques?*

Products may go through multiple inception, sustained sales, and obsolescence phases throughout their life cycle as major upgrades are introduced.

Understanding where a product is in its life cycle can also provide insights into the marketability of the product. If the inception phase of the product was constrained, was that due to the availability of financial resources? If so, then investment dollars may well be able to increase revenues. If, however, the business was constrained by the market (such as a shift in the market to newer technologies) rather than by financial resources, it may indicate a risk area, and the investment dollars might be better applied to other areas such as further strategic planning and infrastructure improvements. The slope of the inception curve can also be constrained if the business is unable to properly project its initial sales or if it is not able to reach agreement with critical vendors and suppliers. *What production volume guarantees has the business given to its suppliers?*

During the sustained sales phase, assuming that the product is competitive, sales will occur on a predictable basis, and there will be a consistent stream of sales (with the exception of normal market fluctuations such as seasonal changes). The price of the product also tends to remain stable during this phase (sales don't require heavy discounting, for instance). It's important to look at the life cycle curve of technology products in particular because of the speed at which these products evolve. Technology products must evolve rapidly in order to remain competitive and viable. *Have product prices remained stable?*

Technology products tend to have a very short shelf life, and they will move through the sustained sales phase quickly if they don't continue to evolve. For many technology products, an 18-month sustained sales period would be a long time. To maintain the value of the product for customers, a business must continually evolve the product by adding new features in order to maintain its price against the competition. Significant upgrades to a product can have the effect of layering one life cycle curve on top of another, extending the life of the product and increasing the number of products sold. You need to assess how quickly the product is evolving and whether this rate is sufficient to support its continuing sales. *Is the product continuing to evolve, or has its development become stagnant?*

During the obsolescence phase, products become less and less competitive due to price or features competition, and sales start to decline at a rapid rate. Basic market economics are reflected by the life cycle curve. The slope of the curve during inception and obsolescence can vary tremendously. Products in obsolescence can still have tremendous investment value. But how can this be? Products take time to become known in the market, and they tend to sell for a long time after customers become familiar them. During obsolescence, the relative costs for maintaining the product are very low.

The obsolescence phase can last a long time. The New York City subway still runs on direct current today, and the last Edison customer using direct current converted to alternating current in 2007! It's a fair assumption that significant investments have not been made in capital improvements or in research and development to evolve the Edison DC system in the prior 50 years while it has continued to generate revenue. At the obsolescence point, there are little or no development costs, and marketing may be accomplished more through word of mouth than through expensive campaigns.

If the obsolescence phase is expected to last over an extended period of time, it may present a real opportunity for investors. There is little or no engineering expense during obsolescence, and production cost drivers, such as volume discounts, are well in place. If the product sold profitably during the sustained sales phase, then its profitability will increase during obsolescence. If the slope of the obsolescence curve indicates that the product will continue to sell for some period of time, even if the overall sales are declining, then there may be an opportunity for investors to consider investing in the business. Estimating how fast sales will fall off can be very risky and difficult to determine. If the strategy is to replace the product before it reaches full obsolescence, than a mitigation strategy for maintaining the product's value may be required. *Will the product reach obsolescence before a replacement can be developed?*

Both risks and opportunities exist throughout a product's life cycle. There may be good investment strategy reasons for investors to capture an opportunity at any point during the product's life cycle. At inception, the entire volume of future product sales revenue becomes available to investors. New products also present investment risks, however. *Does the product work as is, or will it require extensive modification to meet customers' needs?*

During obsolescence there are declining sales volumes and, therefore, potentially lower unit volumes. There can be a risk resulting from higher per unit production costs (product component prices are generally volume based) if the original agreement with the supplier was based on annual sales rather than on total sales. Products that have entered obsolescence, therefore, could be losing their future sales potential if the profit margin resulting from these sales declines. Determining when to *sunset* a product (the point at which it has reached full obsolescence) is important for the business and for the investors. *Is the business able to support the required production volumes needed to make the product profitable?*

PRODUCT DEVELOPMENT
AND PRODUCTION RISKS

In 1999 the explosive growth in the use of cell phones created a large production risk for a business I represented. The business was developing a
product that used electronic components similar to those used in the manufacture of cell phones. Since the phone manufacturers were buying the
components by the millions, our order by contrast was very small to our
suppliers, and we risked being severely backlogged by the supplier for over
a year. Because we recognized the risk early, we were able to implement
a mitigation plan by which we used alternate components that were the
same value but were slightly larger in their physical size than the original
design. The alternate components were too large to be used in cell phones
and therefore were not in demand by the cell phone manufacturers. This
meant we had to change the design of the printed circuit boards to accept
the new component size, but there was plenty of time to accomplish this
and mitigate the risk. *Has the business identified all of the development
and production constraints?*

A continuous risk/opportunity assessment should be conducted of
all products and production methods. If the business follows an institutionalized process for identifying and mitigating risk, it can be a source
of vital information that you can use in your assessment. You'll need to
explore the extent to which the business looks at product development
and production risks to determine whether there is an effective mitigation
strategy in place to avoid identified risks. This is a good place to watch
for the BS Quotient as the business might not be forthcoming with risks
it has previously identified. If the company does have a risk management
plan in place, it would indicate a mature management style. All businesses
encounter risks. The question you are asking is this: How does the company manage risk? *Does the business have a production risk/opportunity
management plan in place?*

THIRD-PARTY PRODUCTS

The use of third-party components in both hardware and software products
is unavoidable. Third-party products are integrated into final (end item)
products for a number of reasons: to improve the development schedule,
to gain access to products that have intellectual property protections such

as patents or copyrights, and to integrate components that the development team members do not have the specific resources to develop themselves. While the use of third-party products may make tremendous sense during development, their use can add risk and legal complexity during an acquisition. All third-party products must be clearly identified and fully licensed for resale.

The terms of any reseller agreement must be clearly defined, and all existing contracts should be reviewed during the legal due diligence. If the investment is an acquisition, third-party licenses may not be transferrable, and there may be an operations risk if these agreements have to be renegotiated. *Have all third-party products been identified, and are they fully licensed by the business?*

There is a "gotcha" effect that businesses should consider if they anticipate a future change of ownership. All third-party agreements must be novated prior to closing if the investment includes a business acquisition. *Are all license agreements with third-party suppliers assignable to the investor if needed?*

Negotiations with vendors and suppliers are often the first place that a pending merger and acquisition (M&A) event becomes exposed beyond the principal parties to the deal. Many third-party vendors, recognizing that the deal may depend on receiving their assignment, will use this as an opportunity to renegotiate their agreement. Care must be used when approaching vendors for assignment agreements. *Are all royalty payments to third-party vendors current and up to date?*

Shareware, freeware, and *open source* are all terms for software components that represent a special category of third-party products. While these components are "free," there are often specific rules that define the terms of their use and that constrain the user when these components are embedded within other products. These terms are a de facto agreement controlling the use of these products that can ultimately constrain how the business sells its product. *Are there any shareware, freeware, open source, or similar components used or embedded within the product? What are they, and what are the terms of their use?*

Products are only as good as their weakest link. This statement applies directly to product quality. The use of third-party products (hardware or software) requires an audit or assessment of the vendor's quality processes. If a product is being developed to high-quality standards and a third-party component is installed that has not been tested to the same standards, then the overall quality of the product will be reduced if that product fails. *How does the business monitor the quality standards of third-party products?*

Summary of the Production Infrastructure Questions

1. Is there a product concept, a working prototype, or a working product?
2. Does the business have the capital equipment it needs in place to support production?
3. Is the production capability of the business sufficient to take the product fully to market?
4. Are demonstration products considered prototypes, or are they actual production units?
5. Is product development on schedule, and have all technical hurdles been overcome?
6. Can the product concept be turned into a salable product **and** make a profit with the planned resources?
7. How far into the production and development process has the core product progressed?
8. Where is the product on the production and development cost curves?
9. Where is the product in its life cycle?
10. Is the business able to keep product deliveries current with its backlog?
11. Does the business have a large uncommitted inventory that it has not been able to sell?
12. Does the business use Lean Manufacturing techniques?
13. What production volume guarantees has the business given to its suppliers?
14. Have product prices remained stable?
15. Is the product continuing to evolve, or has its development become stagnant?
16. Will the product reach obsolescence before a replacement can be developed?
17. Does the product work as is, or will it require extensive modification to meet customers' needs?

18. Is the business able to support the required production volumes needed to make the product profitable?

19. Has the business identified all of the development and production constraints?

20. Does the business have a production risk/opportunity management plan in place?

21. Have all third-party products been identified, and are they fully licensed by the business?

22. Are all license agreements with third-party suppliers assignable to the investor if needed?

23. Are all royalty payments to third-party vendors current and up to date?

24. Are there any shareware, freeware, open source, or similar components used or embedded within the product? What are they, and what are the terms of their use?

25. How does the business monitor the quality standards of third-party products?

CHAPTER 6

Assessment of the Information Management Infrastructure

It's difficult to imagine a business today that doesn't have an extensive computer network in place. My one-person home office has two computers (one being a laptop I take when I travel), a combination printer, scanner, and fax machine all networked wirelessly to share files. My iPhone is also synchronized into this network. I also include a cloud server that allows me to easily access files while I'm on the road. It would be a tremendous understatement to say that all businesses today are information intensive.

Most businesses put as much information into electronic form as possible. It is therefore imperative that your assessment explore the nature of the business's electronically stored information (ESI), including both its online and in-house storage, as well as the systems and processes used to produce, secure, and protect the information. Almost every facet of a business can be automated with computers. The information management infrastructure integrates all of the software applications that support the business plus all of the documents, the internal data control mechanisms, and the data that resides within the system. These are the tools that the business uses to support its operations. The information management system is *not* the same as the products the business produces and sells, and it shouldn't be confused with the products. The information management system integrates the electronic tools, data, and processes that form the backbone of the business. It automates and documents the operational transaction points as work tasks move through the business functions such as HR, security, engineering, accounting, and so on.

Many businesses have an information technology (IT) group whose traditional role is the maintenance of the computers, servers, and other hardware devices and software applications tied to the company's internal network. Some businesses also overload the IT name by referring to their system and software development teams as the "IT department." Throughout *Operations Due Diligence*, I treat the traditional IT role and the role of engineering development groups as separate functions. One focuses on the requirements of the operation's support infrastructure, and the other focuses on the requirements of the product. The terms become overloaded because the software development environment is an infra-structure tool (developers use it to create the product).

The information management system has a much broader scope than the term IT usually implies. The information management system includes the traditional IT function plus the methods and processes used to control the business's operational data (including the operations data-bases and document retention systems). The information management system includes all of the tools, data, policies, and procedures used to support the operation of the business. *Does the business include all soft-ware, data, documents, methods, and processes as part of its information management system?*

> The role of the chief information officer (CIO) should include responsibil-ity for managing the entire information management infrastructure.

The role of the chief information officer (CIO) should include responsibility for managing the entire information management infra-structure. Under this definition, the role of the CIO takes on much more importance. The role of the CIO should not be limited to the more tradi-tional definitions of information technology. The role of the CIO includes responsibility for managing workflow throughout the business. This places much more importance on the role of the CIO as a "process guy" rather than that of a "technology guy." *How does the business define the role of the CIO?*

INFORMATION MANAGEMENT SYSTEM DESIGN

Rube Goldberg was an award-winning cartoonist whose fame grew around his depiction of odd contraptions. A Rube Goldberg design was a collection of things that rolled, fell, twisted or through some intricate series of levers performed a mundane task. Accomplishing a task using a "Rube Goldberg design" is synonymous with applying a complicated, patched-together solution that works only when all of its elements are perfectly aligned. A lot of energy is spent accomplishing even simple tasks. Unfortunately, today's version of a "Rube Goldberg machine" is often the information management system used by many businesses.

When the information management system of a business looks like a Rube Goldberg machine, there may be a risk that the system has become so complex in its combination of applications, patches, and operating procedures that it literally cannot be maintained and also cannot be replaced without an extensive redesign.

The data security system is an example of this. Rather than being implemented by plan and design, in many businesses, it has grown organically through the ad hoc addition of systems without forward planning, and the result is that there's no clear structure behind the specification or design of the information management system. Security becomes a parasite on this system rather than an integral part of it. An integral design is needed to assure efficient operation of the system as well as guaranteeing its security. *Is there an information management system design document that describes the entire system, and is this document kept current?*

The large number of available business applications has resulted in thousands of different file types. In order to integrate the data contained in its information management system, a business must first know and understand what forms the data may take (file formats, media, and so on). *Does the business maintain a list of all of the critical electronic data and the processes used to create and protect the data?*

Identifying the formats used for file and media data storage is also a requirement for determining how to integrate data across multiple information management systems. This can be a real opportunity for cost savings by eliminating the need to enter similar data into multiple systems multiple times. When customers notify the business that they have changed addresses, for instance, does the new address have to be entered separately into the accounts receivable contact management and marketing databases, or are these systems linked to allow the change to be entered once? *Is there an integrated database that supports all activities across the business?*

Supporting multiple operating systems, software applications, and hardware platforms requires staff skilled in each. However, this can be mitigated by establishing standards for the systems the business uses. Deviations from these standards should be made by exception and accompanied by an appropriate rationale for the variance. *Has the business standardized its operating systems, software applications, and/or hardware platforms?*

INFORMATION SECURITY

Information is the blood that runs through the veins of today's businesses. It carries our engineering designs, our accounts receivables, our customer databases, our time sheets, our payrolls, and on and on. The systems that hold our business data require redundant backups and failover protection. Protecting this information requires procedural and physical security as well as electronic security. This includes locked and monitored server and storage rooms and procedures for controlling who has access to electronic data. *What procedural, physical, and logical security protections does the business use to guard its information management system?*

Firewalls and virus detection systems that protect our data have become a way of life. We recognize that, if these protections fail and the data becomes corrupted or becomes exposed beyond our system controls, our business could be disrupted very quickly. The protection of employee and customer data along with our business applications requires a pro-active data security system at all levels of the information management infrastructure. *Does the business have an effective Internet firewall system in place? Does the business have an active (and current) virus protection system in place? Does the business have an effective data security system in place that controls online access permissions and determines who has access to which data?*

INFORMATION MANAGEMENT NETWORK USAGE POLICY

Protecting the information management system from outside intrusion is an absolute necessity today. Most businesses understand this and integrate protection software into their servers. Many fall short, however, when it comes to implementing a network usage policy that provides guidance on both the use of the business's network or the requirements for handling business data (in any form). The business is protected from outside attacks but not from inside attacks from authorized users (like disgruntled employees).

A network usage policy should cover all forms of media including thumb drives, iPods, and personal cell phones that may be connected to the network. All of these devices come with a large storage capacity capable of copying thousands of business documents. The network usage policy needs to clearly state the rights and responsibilities of all users including employees and nonemployees and anyone who is given access to online data. Most businesses ask all users to read and sign a statement that they understand the network usage policy. It's also important for the business to demonstrate its intention to aggressively enforce this policy.

The network usage policy defines the responsibilities of users for handling and protecting business data regardless of the type of media. A list of customers and prospective customers, for instance, whether online in the contact management system, on hard copy at work, at home on a laptop, or on a mobile phone, may have access to private data and must be handled according to the network usage policy. It should be clear to anyone who is given access to this data exactly what is expected of him or her in handling and protecting this data. *Are all information management system users required to sign a network usage policy?*

Many businesses who allow temporary access to guests and visitors fail to segment these temporary users from broad access to their business data. This type of temporary access is often granted for training classes, meetings, and in-house conferences: "Sure, we'd be happy to help you check your e-mail. Here's a key code you can use." *Does the business limit access for temporary network users?*

The rules for use of the information management system need to be clearly defined. This definition covers the way employees use the Internet, their personal e-mail accounts, and their instant messaging accounts from computers that are on the business's network. The rules must protect the business's data in any manner or media under the employees' control. Employees should have clear notice that anything that goes on a business computer belongs to the business and will be monitored. *Have all users been notified that all data that goes over the business's network is legally considered the property of the business and can (and will) be monitored?*

Many businesses give employees open access to the Internet, which can become a gateway for access to games and gaming (gambling), stock monitoring, and political and other message boards, plus lonely hearts and other social networking sites. Aside from the obviously grievous actions such as downloading pornography onto a business computer, there are also other, less grievous, activities that need to be considered by the business and addressed by the network usage policy. In addition, unless the business is prepared to supply the bandwidth for these services, employees may need to be discouraged from accessing sites that provide streaming data such as music, news, video, and stock banners. *Are employees allowed open access to the Internet?*

The use of personal e-mail has also been the subject of a great debate for many businesses. Personal e-mail takes up time and resources, and some managers feel that handling personal e-mail has no more place in a business setting than making extensive personal phone calls from a business phone. If employees have used the business's domain name for their personal e-mail purposes, for personal blogs that mention employees and their titles, or for any other similar Internet-based activities, their communications can show up unexpectedly in web searches and they may not reflect the image the business has worked to establish. Employees' Internet access is not all negative, however. There is also a positive side to granting employees this type of access. Working parents can monitor their children and handle personal business for which they might otherwise have taken time off. Most businesses look at Internet usage as part of their culture, and they consider both sides of the argument when setting their network usage policy and establishing rules to support their policy. *Does the business monitor employee network usage and take a realistic approach to personal Internet usage?*

BASELINE CONTROL

As products continue to be sold, they often continue to evolve through the addition of new features, bug fixes, and cost reduction changes. When a newer, less expensive component or a component changed for some other reason replaces an original, the result is that multiple versions of the product enter production or make it to the market. Consequently, it becomes necessary to track multiple versions of the product. The configuration of each of the released versions can affect pricing and maintenance. An *as-built baseline* needs to be established for each released product. In addition, change control of product baselines is a necessity when there are multiple versions of a product released. Tracking both hardware and software product baselines as well as the documentation used to support them is a function of the information management system. In some cases, it may even be important to track which manufacturing process was used to create different versions of the product.

The information management system will need to include a *configuration management/data management* (CM/DM) *system* that includes version control and tracking functions (such as problem resolution activities, version control, and product serialization). For developmental products, the CM/DM system is used to track which component an engineer has modified and which versions of a printed circuit board or which software subroutines were included in each version of the end product. Software CM/DM systems also track which engineer has "signed out" a particular component so that only one person makes a change at a time. Businesses that don't recognize the need for CM/DM control are operating in a very ad hoc manner and present a significant level of risk to investors: "What version of the software did we send to that customer [who is now having a problem], and how was it tested?" *Does the business have an institutionalized CM/DM baseline control system in place?*

SOFTWARE TOOL LICENSES

Ensuring that all vendor software used by the business is properly and legally licensed is a legal issue, a financial issue, a procedural issue, a policy issue, and an ethics issue that can give you tremendous insight into the business environment you are considering investing in. After all, if the business expects to be paid for its products, it should also expect to pay for other businesses' products that it uses! It amazes me how many people just don't recognize the gravity of this issue. They would never consider shoplifting a published music CD out of a store, but they have no concern about accepting a CD with pirated software from another individual. Theft of software is becoming a large corporate issue, and you need to seriously consider the risk of using pirated products. *Does the business control and audit the software that employees load onto their computers and ensure that it is properly licensed?*

Many software products use *click-through licenses* that require users to perform a mouse click to accept the license during the installation. This requires the users take a positive action that allows the software to load or run. The problem with click-through licenses is that there often isn't even a cursory reading of the license agreement by the users. It becomes a simple "click and go," and the users never actually read the license. This may not be a big issue for a $100 software program, but I've seen the same licensing mechanism used for a $200,000 annual subscription application with an automatic annual renewal clause. That's a pretty significant commitment to make without actually reading the terms of the license! *Does the business regularly review and audit the terms of its vendor software licenses?*

Ensuring that all vendor software used by the business is properly and legally licensed is a legal issue, a financial issue, a procedural issue, a policy issue, and an ethics issue.

Many software license agreements also include *nontransfer clauses*. Transferring ownership of the software tools during an acquisition could create the risk of large inception fees for reassigning these products, or it could put the business in the position of negotiating a new deal with its back against the wall because the investment action has already occurred. *Will there be a cost for reassigning the software development tools during an acquisition?*

DEVELOPMENT AND PRODUCTION TOOLS

The tools needed to support hardware manufacturing or software development are part of the information management system and can present a major cost risk for an investor if the expense hasn't been included as a cost of production (this is an ideal place to watch the BS Quotient!). "Oh sure, we built the prototypes, but we need high-speed machines to support those production volumes."

It's important to understand what type of tool automation will be required to achieve the projected revenue. These costs could be a significant budget item, and they could mean the difference between profitability and failure for some businesses. Tooling costs for plastic parts such as cases can easily run into the hundreds of thousands of dollars before the first component comes out of production. Likewise, an integrated software development environment, needed to support collaboration across even a small software development team, can also cost hundreds of thousands of dollars. *Has the budget accounted for the development and production tool costs and/or the software development environment tool costs?*

Many tools, such as the test equipment used for electronic manufacturing, also require regular maintenance (such as specialized calibration procedures). This type of recurring maintenance cost has to be included in the test department's budget. *Have all of the recurring equipment and calibration costs for hardware tools been budgeted and accounted for?*

Many hardware and software tools require the use of annual maintenance agreements and employee training agreements. These agreements can represent a substantial recurring cost. *Has the budget accounted for the cost of all hardware and software tool maintenance agreements?*

DISASTER RECOVERY AND BUSINESS CONTINUITY

We tend to think of disasters in terms of the attacks on the World Trade Center, Hurricane Katrina, or other mega events. Sometimes, however, less notable events occur that can have a catastrophic effect on a business. In February 1981, an electrical fire in the basement of the State Office Building in Binghamton, New York, spread throughout the basement of the building setting fire to a transformer containing over a thousand gallons of toxin-laden oil. Originally thought to be PCBs, the toxins were soon determined to contain dioxyn and dibenzofuran, two of the most dangerous chemicals ever created. The fire was smoky and quickly filled the

18-story building with smoke. As the transformer burned, the soot entered the building's ventilation shafts and quickly spread toxic soot throughout the building. The building was so badly contaminated that it took 13 years and over $47 million to clean before the building could be reentered or used. Because of the nature of the fire, the building and its contents, including all paper records, computers, and personal effects of the people who worked there, were not recoverable. This type of event would be irrecoverable for many businesses.

Many businesses fail to fully consider the impact a natural or human-caused disaster would have on their operations. What would happen if a fire, flood, or other event occurred that caused an instantaneous interruption of the business's operations? If there were a sudden, true need to restart the business, where would the managers or owners begin? "We back up our computers" and "We keep our backup tapes off site" are the common answers to this question. If the business doesn't have a disaster recovery plan in place to guarantee the continuity of its information management infrastructure, then it may make perfect sense to make this a term of the investment. *Does the business have a disaster recovery plan?*

Disaster recovery is risk management at the extreme.

Disaster recovery is risk management at the extreme. The disaster recovery plan should define how often backups are to be performed and by whom, where the backups will be stored, and the media to be used for the backups. It should also include the specific steps for the restoration of operations after an unplanned shutdown. It took over a year for some of the businesses in New Orleans to restore their operations after Hurricane Katrina. *Does the disaster recovery plan define the requirements for performing network system backups? Does the business have a process for restoring its operations after an emergency?*

Would the business be able to notify its customers who depend on the business as a supplier, about the interruption of service, or would the business be forced to default on its contracts? It takes time, extensive effort, and planning, planning, planning to put a disaster recovery plan in place.

Many businesses have trouble rationalizing the time, effort, and expense it would take to put a true disaster recovery plan in place. They carry insurance, but they haven't considered what the true impact of a full interruption of their business would be. *How would the business retool or replace its stock backlog in time to maintain its production and meet its deliveries following a disaster?*

Most businesses recognize the necessity of regularly backing up their working data so that it can be recovered if necessary. Restoring online data after a disaster, known as *cold starting*, can be a big challenge. Cold-start procedures have to be tested before disaster strikes to ensure that the procedures work when you need them. The recovery of online data is not the only issue that must be addressed. There are well over a thousand federal regulations that require the retention of business documents. The business must be aware of these regulations that govern its information management infrastructure. *Does the business back up its online data (documents, software, and so on), and has the business tested its procedures for restoring the data?*

COMMUNICATIONS SYSTEMS

Looking again at my one-person office, the communications system I use to support my work includes a two-line desk telephone (one line with voice mail for sales and support and one for working discussions) plus a fax line; a mobile phone used when I travel (which also provides me with mobile e-mail); instant messaging and e-mail support; an Internet provider; a website hosting company; a conference telephone account; and an online meeting account. I also send and receive paper mail (although I scan into my computer any documents I will need to be able to search in the future). Paper is still a great communications medium. I guess you could say I'm connected!

There are some admitted overlaps in these services, but each has a specific purpose for my business. If people say they can't reach me, I have to suspect they either didn't try very hard, or they used a carrier pigeon! Communications and access to information are important components of the information management infrastructure of any business. The communications systems for my small business have grown organically with each function being added as the need was recognized. I can get away with this in my office, but this is not possible for most small businesses where employees share services. *Does the business have an integrated communications plan, or has its communications infrastructure grown organically? Is the current communications system sufficient to meet the foreseeable needs of the business?*

Communications systems are expensive, but there is often an opportunity for savings if these systems have grown organically. Communications system costs include the connectivity from various service providers and the expense of the equipment. If the business has implemented its communications system organically, it may also have expenses due to the inefficiencies of employees trying to learn to use multiple systems (and potentially misusing them for nonbusiness purposes). All of these inefficiencies can be converted to opportunities. A negotiation with the service vendors is usually a good starting point. Telecommunications plans change on a very frequent basis and are highly competitive. *Does the business identify and manage all communications expenses? Are there opportunities to consolidate or reduce communications expenses?*

Summary of the Information Management Infrastructure Questions

1. Does the business include all software, data, documents, methods, and processes as part of its information management system?
2. How does the business define the role of the CIO?
3. Is there an information management system design document that describes the entire system, and is this document kept current?
4. Does the business maintain a list of all of the critical electronic data and the processes used to create and protect the data?
5. Is there an integrated database that supports all activities across the business?
6. Has the business standardized on operating systems, software applications, and/or hardware platforms?
7. What procedural, physical, and logical security protections does the business use to guard its information management system?

8. Does the business have an effective Internet firewall system in place?
9. Does the business have an active (and current) virus protection system in place?
10. Does the business have an effective data security system in place that controls online access permissions and determines who has access to which data?
11. Are all information management system users required to sign a network usage policy?
12. Does the business limit access for temporary network users?
13. Have all users been notified that all data that goes over the business's network is legally considered the property of the business and can (and will) be monitored?
14. Are employees allowed open access to the Internet?
15. Does the business monitor employee network usage and take a realistic approach to personal Internet usage?
16. Does the business have an institutionalized CM/DM baseline control system in place?
17. Does the business control and audit the software that employees load onto their computers and ensure that it is properly licensed?
18. Does the business regularly review and audit the terms of its vendor software licenses?
19. Will there be a cost for reassigning the software development tools during an acquisition?
20. Has the budget accounted for the development and production tool costs and/or the software development environment tool costs?
21. Have all of the recurring equipment and calibration costs for hardware tools been budgeted and accounted for?
22. Has the budget accounted for the cost of all hardware and software tool maintenance agreements?
23. Does the business have a disaster recovery plan?
24. Does the disaster recovery plan define the requirements for performing network system backups?
25. Does the business have a process for restoring its operations after an emergency?

26. How would the business retool or replace its stock backlog in time to maintain its production and meet its deliveries following a disaster?
27. Does the business back up its online data (documents, software, and so on), and has the business tested its procedures for restoring the data?
28. Does the business have an integrated communications plan, or has its communications infrastructure grown organically?
29. Is the current communications system sufficient to meet the foreseeable needs of the business?
30. Does the business identify and manage all communications expenses?
31. Are there opportunities to consolidate or reduce communications expenses?

CHAPTER 7

Assessment of the Sales and Marketing Infrastructure

In 1919 Edsel Ford succeeded his father, Henry, as president of the Ford Motor Company. During his tenure, Edsel Ford made a number of contributions to the business, the most notable of which was the addition of the Lincoln Mercury division. His tenure ended with his early death in 1943 at the age of 49 after which his son, Henry Ford II, assumed the presidency. In 1957, Ford memorialized Edsel with the launch of a new product line in his name. The launch of the Edsel division represented a major marketing initiative for the Ford Motor Company.

The Edsel was intended to compete with the General Motors mid-priced Oldsmobile. Until that point the Lincoln Mercury had competed with Oldsmobile, but Ford hoped to change the persona of Lincoln by creating an upscale image for it that would be able to compete with the Cadillac. Ford launched a massive promotion in 1957 to introduce the new Edsel. The promotion featured all kinds of incentives, even offering all new buyers a chance to win a live pony. The print and television advertising for the promotion was excessive and successful: the public was made very aware of the launch of the new product, and great market expectations were created for the new cars.

While Ford succeeded in creating high expectations for the Edsel, the car failed to live up to Ford's promises, and the Edsel was quickly recognized as a dismal failure. Ford had clearly failed to understand the market, and it had underestimated the resources that would be needed to launch the new product line. Ford had overpromised and overreached. The product was advertised as something different and special, and Ford wasn't able to meet these expectations.

The Edsel product line lasted only two years, and Ford finally discontinued production with the 1960 model. There was an economic recession at the time that contributed to the demise of the Edsel, which had been priced higher than the competition in a poor market. The failure of the Edsel was so bad that its name has become synonymous with failed products. Ford miscalculated the risks associated with launching a new product line, and the quality of the Edsel, often shipped with missing parts, became a significant factor in its demise. Ford was not able to manage its distribution channel, and when the Edsel failed, so did many of the dealerships that had planned to support and sell it. Consumers said they found the car grotesque compared to the competition, which had moved to a slicker, sportier styling. The front end of the Edsel looked odd, publicly stated to look "like a vagina" (clearly not acceptable by 1950s' standards).

Ford had started the design of the Edsel at a time when bigger was better, and the resulting vehicle was massive. By the time the Edsel was actually offered, the market trend had changed toward smaller vehicles (by 1957 standards). In its desire to enter the midpriced market, Ford had failed to strategically plan at almost every step. The people on the Ford development team failed to recognize the market shift when they conducted their market analysis; they failed to strategically plan their manufacturing resources; they failed to correctly plan their distribution channels; they failed to predict the market trends in price or appearance; they failed to provide proper support for the product; and they failed to deliver on the expectations their marketing team had created. The result was that Ford lost an estimated $350 million as a direct result of their lack of strategic planning and effective market analysis. Virtually every facet of the business had failed to produce a salable product. *Are there sales and marketing process improvements that would increase the opportunities for product sales?*

The sales and marketing infrastructure provides the framework that aligns and coordinates the activities of all employees with the goals of the business: to sell products and make a profit.

Sustainable businesses take the time to plan and design their sales and marketing infrastructure, and by doing so, they are choosing to follow a systemic approach that will guide all of their activities toward the generation of revenue. The engineer who finds a creative way to build a product, the tester who verifies that the product meets its quality requirements, the support representative who helps solve a customer's problem, and the accounts receivable clerk who works with a customer to process a payment are all contributing elements of the sales and marketing infrastructure. Sustainable businesses improve the sales and marketing infrastructure on a continuing basis. *Is there a coordinated sales and marketing strategy that spans the business?*

By institutionalizing their sales and marketing infrastructure, the business is creating a culture of selling. All employees become responsible for helping the business identify its customer needs and sell its products. One of the claims I hear businesses make quite often is: "All of our employees are expected to be salespeople." Successful businesses know that all of the employees have a role in sales, even if they never meet the customer and never personally speak with the end users. *Do all employees understand that "doing that little bit extra" for a customer helps make sales?*

"All of our employees are expected to be salespeople."

The sales and marketing infrastructure crosses all organizational boundaries and focuses the staff toward selling products and making a profit. The salesperson on the street is only the "tip of the spear." To engage their entire staff, many businesses conduct regular "state-of-the-business meetings" that inform all employees about the goals of the business and their individual importance to the business's overall success. *Does the business conduct periodic state-of-the-business discussions with the employees to explain how the business is doing with its sales?*

MARKETING

The marketing function provides the strategic direction that keeps the business on the correct course for growth. It defines the market, positions the business into that market, and identifies the optimal product for the market, while moving the business ahead of its competition.

Before you begin to assess the sales and marketing infrastructure, you will have to do your market homework to establish a baseline from which to assess the marketing efforts of the business. Performing your own market research will give you a level of market awareness that will enable you to determine the effectiveness of the business's marketing activities. If the business doesn't track market trends, for instance, it could be at risk of losing its ability to sell due to unanticipated shifts in the market. Your market research will allow you to understand these potential risks. An undercapitalized business, which lacks the resources to fully conduct market research or advertise its products, could represent either a tremendous risk or a great opportunity for an investor who is ready to add the additional capital. *Is the business at any risk of losing its ability to sell?*

When the Ford Motor Company launched a full-out marketing campaign that advertised the Edsel, it was trying to attract any person who would potentially buy one of its automobiles. The approach of the marketing group should be like fishing with a net rather than fishing with a line. The marketing group puts chum in the water to attract a school of hungry fish closer to the boat. These are the fish who are truly interested and who are most likely to bite. The marketing group is responsible for "chumming" the market to attract the leads that are most likely to purchase the product. This starts with the creation of the public's brand awareness of the product. To accomplish this, the marketing group creates a public persona that the market will associate with the business. This persona becomes a brand that the market will use to identify the business. *Has the business established a recognizable brand image in the market?*

To continue my fishing analogy, the goal isn't to pull in one customer; it's to pull in as many customers as possible. As simple as this analogy may seem, it's surprising how often businesses implement a singular rather than a plural marketing approach by spending their time and money going after that one big client. Instead of following an ad hoc approach to marketing through which the business pursues individual opportunities, successful businesses follow a strategic plan that identifies where the bulk of the market demand is expected to be. They then attempt to position their businesses to sell products into that broader market space. The primary reason many businesses fail to reach out to as wide a market as possible is that the marketing budget constrains them and limits their reach. It's much less expensive to chase individual opportunities than to reach out to a wide market. *Does the business have a sufficient marketing budget?*

By chasing individual opportunities, the business becomes defocused from its strategic goal, which can have a snowball effect on the way it operates the business. When the focus of the business becomes providing a solution to meet the needs of one customer, it may not spend the time or resources needed to develop a solution that meets the needs of the larger market.

Chasing an individual customer is a risk because it consumes resources and causes missed opportunities. It's easy for a business to fall into the "one-customer" trap, particularly young businesses that are hungry for revenue. As the business drifts away from its strategic plan, it starts to chase the market rather than lead the market. The business spends its time fighting to catch up to their competition rather than letting the competition chase them. "The competition added this new feature so now we need to stop doing what we had planned to do so we can add a similar feature." Businesses that lead the market do so through innovation and the development of disruptive technologies and solutions, not by chasing their competition. *Does the business lead the market, or is it becoming defocused by following individual or discrete opportunities?*

When the business first introduces a new or rapidly evolving technology, the market for the product may be immature. In these cases the marketing group may need to take an active role in educating potential customers about the advantages of the new technology and demonstrating the benefits offered by the new product. Customers often have a need, but they are not aware that a solution exists, or in some cases, they may not even realize the need until it's pointed out. In these cases, the marketing group is creating the customer demand for the product by educating the market. They're chumming the water! *Has marketing created a demand for the product?*

MARKET AWARENESS

The business can have the best product available at the lowest cost, but if customers are not aware of the product, they can't buy it. The market has to be made aware of the business and its products. The ability of a business to establish a presence in the market is most often controlled by the size of its marketing budget. There are many tools available for creating market awareness, but the budget constrains which tools the business will be able to employ.

Market Awareness Tools

Websites
Press releases
Print and electronic media advertising
Social media advertising
Industry working groups
Conferences and papers
Customer training seminars
E-mail and direct mail advertising
Telemarketing
Word-of-mouth referrals
Other

Websites have become the electronic billboards for virtually all industries and an absolute necessity for any business. Although websites can be created very inexpensively, establishing an effective marketing strategy that addresses the role of the website can quickly drive these costs up. Websites have become far more than a billboard signpost. They are the business's online catalog, its point-of-sale terminal, its classroom, its news outlet, its interactive customer communications tool, and much more. *Does the business include a website in its marketing strategy?*

When a business wants to make a public announcement about such newsworthy events as the release of a new product, a change in its location, a change in its leadership, or its financial performance, it announces this "news" by issuing a press release. A *press release* is an official communication from the business to a communications media outlet such as newspapers, magazines, trade journals, or electronic Internet-based media interested in news about the market. Press releases are often one-time events, but they are also used to support marketing campaigns with multiple strategic announcements. *Does the business regularly issue press releases as part of its marketing strategy?*

Print and electronic media advertising is used to reach broad target audiences. This type of advertising is generally expensive, and it requires careful design and media placement. *Does the business use print and electronic media advertising as part of its marketing strategy?*

Social media networking has rapidly gained acceptance as an inter-active marketing tool. Social media sites, including Facebook, LinkedIn, Twitter, and industry blogs, are inexpensive to set up but labor intensive to maintain. Businesses that incorporate social media into their marketing plan must develop a marketing strategy and follow it closely. Social media strategies allow the business to reach a highly targeted audience, but that audience has to agree to be contacted. Customers must agree to friend, link, join groups, or follow the business or the market in some manner. Nevertheless, social media networking is a great way to generate recurring business with existing customers. It also makes it easier for a business to identify interested customer user groups for up-selling and announcing special sales. *Does the business use social media networking as part of its marketing strategy?*

Many *industry working groups* bring business experts together for activities like standards developments. These groups may include spon-sors from different parts of the same industry such as suppliers or vendors, manufacturers, channel sales groups, and even some users. By participat-ing in these groups, the business is presenting itself as an industry expert. Creating market awareness by participating in this type of group is a good way to generate referral business. One of the risks to be cautious of in this environment, however, is exposing skilled employees to competitors who may also be participating and may be looking for new talent. *Does the business participate in industry working groups as part of its marketing strategy?*

Similar to participating in industry working groups (and often in conjunction with them) is attending industry *conferences* and presenting *papers* there. Attending can be done passively by simply sending employ-ees to the conference, or it can be done aggressively by becoming a sponsor or paying to have a display booth. In some industries this type of participa-tion is an absolute necessity. By encouraging employees to present papers at industry conferences, the business is again making a statement that it brings a high level of expertise to the market. *Does the business partici-pate in industry shows and conferences as part of its marketing strategy?*

By offering *customer training seminars and webinars* (online semi-nars), the business is reaching out to educate potential customers. This is a highly effective way to introduce new technology and concepts so as to build new markets for the business. Webinars are cost effective, but they do not allow direct contact with potential customers. For high-end products, I have occasionally had a sales representative sit through a webinar at the customer's facility with the customer to "see which way their eyes rolled"! *Does the business conduct customer training seminars and webinars as part of its marketing strategy?*

E-mail and direct mail advertising is used in some industries where a highly targeted audience can be identified. This can be effective when customers have signed up to receive product notifications, but it can also be a risk when seen as spam or junk mail that does little more than annoy potential customers. *Does the business use e-mail or direct mail advertising as part of its marketing strategy?*

Telemarketing, making direct phone calls to potential customers, is also used in some industries. It is a shot gun approach to a very broad market generally targeted to specific demographic audiences. This type of marketing is often not received well, and its use should be considered carefully. *Does the business use telemarketing as part of its marketing strategy?*

The best market awareness tool, in terms of cost and effectiveness comes from satisfied customers telling other potential customers how satisfied they are and how much they benefited from the business. This type of advertising should not be left to chance. Customers should be incentivized to "spread the word." This is done through the use of loyalty programs, referral discounts, and other benefits that encourage *word-of-mouth referrals*. *Does the business incentivize word-of-mouth referrals as part of its marketing strategy?*

The effectiveness of all of these market awareness tools is dependant on the characteristics of the target market, and decisions about which to use are tied to the available budget resources.

Your assessment needs to explore how the business uses market awareness tools for its advertising and how it measures the effectiveness of each tool. The list provided here can be expanded to include any other valid methods used by the business.

Exploring the constraints that have limited the businesses choice of marketing tools is a good way to understand both the resource limitations and the creativity of the business. For instance, if the business hasn't used print advertising, has that decision been based on the cost of using this media? Or does the business have other reasons to believe this marketing tool won't work in its industry? If the budget wasn't the only constraint when selecting market awareness tools, than exploring the rationale behind the choices may disclose additional opportunities to generate sales leads by revising the rationale. *What rationale is used for selecting marketing awareness tools?*

CONTACT MANAGEMENT SYSTEM

Communication among and across the sales and marketing infrastructure is critical to customer satisfaction and retention and, consequently, to recurring sales. Customer contact reports are commonly used to document interactions with customers and to inform other staff members about those interactions. Reviewing the contact management system (CMS) is another way to assess the sales qualification process. If the business doesn't use a CMS, you may have found an area for further discovery, depending on the business's sales model (broad retail sales to the general public may not require contact lists, for instance, but the retail sales may require a list of distributors). Again, the business will need to be very cautious here if the due diligence is being conducted by a competitor, and, if you are a strategic investor, you may need to understand the business's resistance to allowing you access to its CMS. *Does the business use a contact management system?*

MARKET ANALYSIS

Many times, businesses rely on informal methods for collecting market data. "I just heard from someone that this just happened to that competitor." This type of market data is largely hearsay and is coming from the rumor mill rather than a valid analysis of the market. This is an area where you need to be wary, challenge answers and explore the assessment responses in detail. A response that says "Our prices are the lowest in the market" or "We have the market-leading solution" should be met with the response: "How do you know?" *What is the source of the business's market information, and how current is this data?*

Sustainable businesses don't rely on the rumor mill when making strategic decisions because they recognize that this data is not sufficiently reliable to change their strategic direction. Strategic decisions should result from continuous market analysis and study of the market trends. A market analysis can be conducted either internally or by an outside consultant; however, independence in this area is often a good idea. Businesses develop a bias based on their past market experiences or the past experiences of their employees, and this bias can skew the results of an internal analysis. "When I worked over there five years ago, they decided not to go into this market." Things change over time in response to competition and other market factors, and it is always difficult to identify the validity or timing of the rumor mill. Because the business operates in the market, it develops a view of the market that might not match its customers' or competitors' view. On the other hand, the market knowledge the business holds may not be reproducible by an independent entity, such as a consulting firm, who doesn't work regularly in the market trenches. *Who conducted the market analysis, and how valid is it today?*

Watch the BS Quotient when discussing the business's market position; in particular, listen for the "I [or we] feel" statement. "We feel we will be able to completely capture this market segment." "Oh really, based on what?" Also remember that if this is a strategic acquisition, the business will expose a lot of market intelligence during the due diligence. Businesses preparing for a due diligence should always keep this in mind. If you are a strategic investor, you might want to review the terms of your NDA (and your ethics policy) at this point.

Determining what the real market perceptions are of the business can be difficult, but it is important for you to do so for two reasons. First, it gives you the opportunity to hear the business state what it thinks the market perception of it is. Second, you will be able to compare this to the actual market perception (as you have identified it). The difference in these perceptions is an indicator of the effectiveness of the business's marketing ability. Knowing what the current customers are telling others about the business provides a clue to where the strategic path of the business lies. And it can go two ways: "Wow, the company's new product incorporated a real disruptive technology that made our job much easier for us." Or, "I can't believe it. We waited for the company's new product, and when it finally came out, it was already behind the rest of the industry." *What is the public persona of the business? Is the actual perception of the market consistent with the persona that marketing is trying to create?*

A misalignment between the image the marketing group is trying to create for the business and the actual market perception of customers is also a risk indicator. "We think the product is easy to use because we work with it all the time, but customers keep saying it's too complex for them." Sometimes there is a benefit from conducting an internal (and anonymous) market survey. If the same survey is performed with customers and employees, the results can be compared to identify these misalignments. "Customers give us good grades for product support, but our support staff wants to add staff to improve our response time." Ideally the employees will be more critical of the business than the customers. *Why did the customer choose this business over the competition?*

The market analysis you conduct in preparation for the due diligence should also include a competitive analysis that includes an assessment of the businesses reputation for usable, reliable, affordable products. I'm cautious when I hear a business claim that it "leads the market" or that it is "the only one" in a market. This type of market lead generally doesn't last for long. I'd much rather hear, "There are other businesses in the market, and here are the discriminators that will help capture our share of the market." This means the business found a way to create product value by making the product more useful, more reliable or less expensive than the competition. *Has the business conducted a recent competitive analysis?*

A competitive analysis is another task that is best performed by an independent entity. There are just too many pressures on internal marketing staff members for them to perform an unbiased competitive analysis. For example, the marketing manager may be biased because he doesn't want to tell his boss that someone else is better or that the prior market analysis led the business to develop the wrong product. By its nature, a competitive analysis tends to put people on the defensive, and this makes it difficult to conduct in-house. *Has the competitive analysis been verified externally, or does it reflect an unjustified bias toward the business?*

STRATEGIC PLANNING

The old *Newhart* show (CBS, 1982 to 1990) had a couple of characters who ran a business called "Anything for a Buck." This wasn't the type of business most investors would be interested in, but it resembled many businesses that operate without a clearly defined road map. One of the recommendations I regularly make to clients when I start working with them is to either take the time to create a strategic road map or change their name to "Anything for a Buck!" It's easy to become defocused by chasing near-term revenues.

"But all revenues are good revenues, right?" The problem with this is the risk that chasing near-term revenues will divert resources from completing the strategic activities required to achieve the long-term goals of the business. Sustainable businesses keep on track through the rigorous execution of their strategic plan. If a business makes a tactical decision to divert from its strategic plan, than it needs to make a conscious decision to modify the plan based on its changed long-term goals rather than moving from the unique needs of one customer to another. *How does the business establish a strategic plan for its products, and how well does it follow this plan?*

Marketing provides the "radar" a business uses to guide its strategic planning (Figure 7.1). This radar is the result of the insights gained by performing a continuous market analysis. The strategic plan, often represented as a strategic road map, identifies the critical drivers and current trends that indicate where the market is headed in the future. It is the radar that guides the business along a path similar to the market. Many times

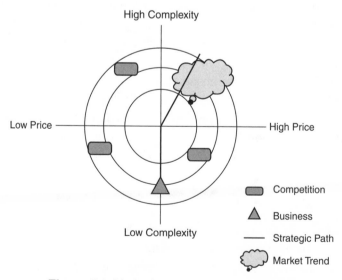

Figure 7.1 Marketing as a Business's Radar

businesses navigate through the market with only speculation and rumor rather a strategy founded on real market intelligence data. Without gathering valid market data, the business risks committing resources to develop the wrong product. *Does the business follow a strategic plan that guides its future direction in the market?*

The strategic plan starts with a solid understanding of the current market position and a clear definition of where the business wants to go. The plan is implemented by assessing the financial targets and constraints of the business (What are the revenue goals, and what investment will the business require to achieve them?); the technology goals and schedule that must be achieved (Will achieving the strategic plan mean developing some breakthrough intellectual property?); the revised support requirements (Do new customer training programs need to be developed?); and the organizational dependencies that must be overcome (Do the employees have the correct skills to execute the plan?). Establishing the starting position for a strategic plan is a great reason to perform a self-assessment. *How well does the strategic direction of the business align with the direction of the market?*

Sustainable businesses keep two thoughts in mind when executing their strategic plan. First, evolving technology can change markets at a very fast rate, and second, new technologies take time to develop. For technology businesses in particular, these facts require that a business be willing to adjust the strategic plan in response to changes in the market. The risk is that markets are a moving target. If the market changes direction suddenly, the business risks not having the time to react, and it may continue on the wrong path by developing a product that will not be relevant by the time it's delivered. There needs to be a balance between chasing customers and following the strategic plan. The direction of the business should be changed only after the strategic plan changes, and frequent changes to the strategic plan need to be avoided. Changes that are made too often indicate that the market and competitive analysis may not have been performed effectively. *How frequently does the business change its strategic plan?*

PRODUCT MANAGEMENT

Businesses are frequently founded by individuals who started with only a vision of a particular business or its products. As the business grows and diversifies, that vision needs to be passed on to other individuals with the responsibility for maintaining the future vision of the business. Product management must carry the responsibility for maintaining the vision needed to evolve the product. Products need to continually evolve to remain competitive, or they risk stagnation and early obsolescence. "I was the first person to introduce this product to the market, and we sold a lot of them. Now everyone is making them, and we are fighting to stay ahead of the pack."

The product manager's function supplements the visionary's function, and the product manager has the formal responsibility for maintaining the future vision and strategic plan for a product. Product management replaces the dependence on a single visionary. Relying solely on an individual who has the "knack for predicting where the market is heading" and for leading product development in that direction comes with some risks. The original visionary is often the principal or a key staff member of the business. If this is an acquisition, will the visionary remain? Will the visionary be leaving and possibly compete with the business in the future? Does the visionary plan to retire? Formalizing the role of the visionary by establishing a product management function allows the individual visionary to exit if desired. *Does the business have a person who is the visionary, and how has the visionary's participation in the business been secured for the future?*

Products evolve through modifications and updates. Existing customers are usually eager to describe changes they want in derivative products. The product manager is responsible for listening to customers and creating opportunities for them to provide feedback. This is a great source of gathering real market intelligence. *Does the business have a formalized process for collecting customer feedback as part of its product management?*

Participation in activities, such as industry working groups, conference committees, and standards groups, is another good way for product management to maintain the product vision. The business's level of participation in these industry events and the types of contributions the business makes to the industry are additional indicators of how current the business remains with the market. *What industry working groups, conference committees, or standards groups does the business participate in to remain current with the market?*

SALES

If the business has developed a visionary product based on a disruptive new technology and is offering this product at a highly profitable competitive price in unlimited volumes, then it should be easy to make sales. In fact, customers should be knocking on the door demanding more products from the business. And who wouldn't want to invest in this business! The sales process is easy in this case. Open the door, have the customers form a line, and take their orders. If things aren't going quite that smoothly, then the sales and marketing infrastructure will need to be optimized to produce sustaining sales.

The Sales Process

The sales team leads the revenue collection activities of the business. It is responsible for managing customers; educating and training customers about the products; sustaining relationships with customers; and establishing price and value for the product to maximize profit from each sale. Once the water has been chummed by the marketing group, it's the job of the sales team to pull the fish into the boat.

The goal of marketing is to provide a continuous list of qualified sales leads. These are the hungry fish. The sales team now systematically processes these leads until they are converted into paying customers. *Does the business follow a defined sales process?*

The sales process has been the subject of hundreds of books. These books typically promote a new selling theory or a new tool that automates part of the sales process. My goal here isn't to endorse one sales method over another. The sales process the business implements needs to follow a model that best supports sales of the product. Sales methods can range from the low-priced, high-volume types of products that are sold off "J hooks" in retail stores, or they can be low-volume, high-priced "one-of-a-kind" solutions. Sales models can rely on direct sales, whereby the business sells its products directly to the end users, or they can rely on indirect sales, whereby the business works through its channel partners to make sales to the end users. Products can be very low tech, requiring a low level of product support, or they can be complex, requiring a high level of product support. The business should have considered all of these factors when establishing its sales model. *Can the business explain its sales model and defend the rationale behind it?*

Sustainable businesses follow a repeatable sales process rather than relying on an ad hoc approach. Like all other operations processes, the sales process has to be continuously improved. Those things that work are continually optimized, and those that don't work are dropped. If a salesperson realizes that telling prospects about an industry quality award a product just received helps to close sales, this information needs to be passed on to the entire sales team so that everyone else also mentions the award. Over time, the efficiency of the sales process will improve. Successful sales teams use metrics, such as closure rates, to track and improve the performance of the sales process. *Has the efficiency of the sales process improved over time?*

The sales process is often referred to as a *pipeline* or *funnel* that can be monitored as a continuous flow of sales leads from the market, some percentage of which are eventually converted into sales. The process institutionalizes the steps for converting raw sales leads into closed sales. Managing the sales process requires tracking sales leads through each step of the process and identifying and maximizing the opportunity for the eventual sale. The advantage of monitoring the sales process in this manner is that it gives the business the ability to measure progress to determine the effectiveness of each step of the process. *How does the business monitor and measure its sales pipeline results?*

Problems arise in the sales process when it becomes difficult to account for all of the variables in the process. Occasionally, there is so much subjectivity in the process that no meaningful performance measure can be established. Predicting how many leads will make it all the way through the process or how long that might take cannot be accurately predicted. Normal market fluctuations can affect the flow of leads and make it difficult to assign any statistical significance to the sales metrics. Some potential customers may be in a hurry to purchase, and some may want to take their time. This makes it difficult to establish valid sales metrics like the percent of leads converted to sales or the length of the average sales cycle (time from beginning to end). If projections are based on an expected closure time, then these projections may not be met. The risk is not achieving a sufficient number of sales leads to establish statistical significance in the conversion numbers. With no valid metric established, the sales model is unreliable. When this happens, managing the sales process by looking only at the metrics may be more of an art than a science, and other approaches need to be used to establish valid projections. *What is the conversion ratio from leads to prospects and from prospects to customers? Is there statistical significance in the accuracy of these numbers?*

Establishing a sales process that is repeatable and reliable requires more than just looking at the sales metrics, particularly during product inception when the numbers of sales are low. As sales volumes grow, the opportunity for true metric management also grows. When the volume is sufficient for tracking sales metrics, managers need to assess the activities being used to close individual leads ("What actions are you using to close this lead?") rather than focusing strictly on metrics like closure rates ("You've been talking to this prospect for three months. Why hasn't it been closed yet?"). Management flexibility is required due to the potential variances in the process, particularly during product inception. During your assessment, the sales metrics may not be as relevant as asking how each of the leads that support the forecast will be managed. You must understand the method being used in order to understand the validity of the projections. *Does the business focus on managing individual leads, or does it make decisions based on feedback from sales metrics?*

Assessing Customers

One way to assess exactly where the business stands in the market is to talk to existing customers. This is an important assessment activity, but it must be done with caution, particularly if the business relies on recurring sales. The rumor of an acquisition or sale of the business could put these sales at risk. An additional problem occurs when the business and investor are bound by a mutual nondisclosure agreement. This would preclude contact with customers who are considered third parties unless the contact is agreed to in advance (or unless the contact is specifically granted by the nondisclosure agreement). Exposing an acquisition to a customer too soon can be a risk, and it has to be handled with caution.

The business will of course be tempted to provide a list of customers who it knows will give a favorable report. You will want to obtain a complete customer listing so that you can independently determine which customers to speak with (after first notifying the business). The list should include all current customers, as well as past customers who no longer use the product. This is an area where full cooperation between the parties is called for and where creativity needs to be shown to avoid premature market rumors of an M&A event.

Questions can be posed to customers in the form of an independent market analysis, or information can be requested by the business in the form of a customer survey that you provide. This can be accomplished as part of your market and competitive analysis. This is another risk area for the business if the due diligence is being performed as part of a strategic acquisition by a competitor. Both parties need to have a clear understanding of the goals and methods to be used when speaking with current customers, and the use of an independent third party may be called for to protect the business as well as the investor. *Is there a list of current and past customers?*

Assessing Sales Prospects

During your due diligence, the business will want to tell you about all of its great sales prospects and use these as evidence to validate its long-term sales projections. If the business's claims are based on pending deal closings, that's great news, but it's important to explore beyond these claims to understand the business's ability to sell beyond these immediate prospects. Watch the BS Quotient here! Maybe these prospects are just the "low hanging fruit." Are the projections still valid after these near-term sales have been closed? *Are the sales projections based on the closure of sales to specific customers, or do they reflect an effective long-term strategy?*

Prospects are leads that have been qualified as having a genuine interest and ability to purchase a product. As you begin to assess the sales process, you may be told about specific prospects that were used to validate the forecasts. You need to determine how these prospects were qualified. You need to keep the BS Quotient low by using the data supplied by the business to independently construct your own version of the sales pipeline. *How does the business qualify its sales leads to validate them as sales prospects?*

You should never ask to meet with potential customers. You don't want to be responsible or liable for scaring off a prospective customer.

It's not a good practice to ask for permission to meet with potential customers in order to validate the sales pipeline. You don't want to be responsible or liable for scaring off a prospective customer. One way to resolve this is to validate the sales qualification process and build confidence in the businesses sales process.

Sales Territories

In medieval times, feudal lords (patrons) would grant parcels of land to subjects (vassals) as repayment for their loyalty. The vassals would make their living by working the land and retaining a portion of the crops they grew for their patrons. The fiefdoms were grants, allowing the vassals to work the patrons' land. Occasionally, for reasons only the patrons could decide, the vassals lost their grants and had to seek a living elsewhere. This occasionally resulted in the vassals getting together to burn torches and angrily march on the castle! Today's version of the fiefdom is the grant from a business to its salespeople allowing them to sell its products into a specified territory. The salespeople earn a commission by working the territory (the salespeople become vassals under the patronage of the business).

The subject of sales territories can be an emotional one for the sales representatives. They often consider their sales territories endowed fiefdoms, and they believe they have earned perpetual rights to the sales territories. The sales representatives work hard to build and maintain their customer relationships within their territories, and their commissions directly reflect how well they have done their job. Occasionally, for reasons the business decides are necessary, such as merging sales territories following an M&A event, salespeople are asked to change their sales territory. They respond by burning the business's catalog and marching on the HR department of a competitor taking their developed relationships along with them. Changing sales territories is a risk. *Are there any plans to change sales territories?*

If the investment plan calls for restructuring sales territories, care must be used because this risks breaking established customer relationships and potentially seeing them move to a competitor. Restructuring sales territories can pose a risk to an investor whose plan is to integrate the members of a sales team into an existing organization or who wants to increase sales by adding additional sales representatives to existing territories. Many businesses take the position that sales territories belong to the business and the sales representatives have been given a license to mine the territories. The business reserves the right to change or restructure territories at any time. Having the right to change territories, however, doesn't always mean it's the smartest move! Established relationships have to be changed with extreme caution, consideration, and preparation. A risk mitigation strategy should be carefully thought out when territory changes are anticipated. *How does the business manage its sales territories and allocate the sales representatives' rights to mine these territories?*

Territories controlled by channel partners should be clearly defined by a reseller agreement and established contractually as sales territories. The business should have a plan for managing the performance of its channel partners if it is going to grant them dedicated territories. Without performance and term limits, these territories can become dormant and therefore a risk to the business due to lost sales in the territory. An alternate model is to never guarantee territories to channel partners. The problem with this model is that the channel partners will have very little incentive to advertise the business's products within territories they can't control. Also, in these cases, the tendency is to believe that the more resellers the better and to sign almost anyone who asks to be a channel partner. This can be risky for two reasons. The first is that there may be resellers who aren't qualified to represent the product who can damage the business's reputation. The second is that true channel partners require training and support, and the cost of this training must be offset by the sales revenue they produce. *How does the business qualify its channel partners?*

If the business provides continuing sales support and has to get involved often to help channel partners complete sales, then the business, which may have greatly discounted the cost of each sale to the channel partners, is still doing the work to close the sales. The business might have been better off using a direct sale method or paying lead referral fees and eliminating the channel partners altogether. Channel partners require significant training to allow them to complete sales without hands-on support from the business. *What type of training and support does the business provide for its channel partners?*

Summary of the Sales and Marketing Infrastructure Questions

1. Are there sales and marketing process improvements that would increase the opportunities for product sales?
2. Is there a coordinated sales and marketing strategy that spans the business?
3. Do all employees understand that "doing that little bit extra" for a customer helps make sales?
4. Does the business conduct periodic state-of-the-business discussions with the employees to explain how the business is doing with its sales?
5. Is the business at any risk of losing its ability to sell?
6. Has the business established a recognizable brand image in the market?
7. Does the business have a sufficient marketing budget?
8. Does the business lead the market, or is it becoming defocused by following individual or discrete opportunities?
9. Has marketing created a demand for the product?
10. Does the business include a website in its marketing strategy?
11. Does the business regularly issue press releases as part of its marketing strategy?
12. Does the business use print and electronic media advertising as part of its marketing strategy?
13. Does the business use social media networking as part of its marketing strategy?
14. Does the business participate in industry working groups as part of its marketing strategy?
15. Does the business participate in industry shows and conferences as part of its marketing strategy?
16. Does the business conduct customer training seminars and webinars as part of its marketing strategy?
17. Does the business use e-mail or direct mail advertising as part of its marketing strategy?
18. Does the business use telemarketing as part of its marketing strategy?
19. Does the business incentivize word-of-mouth referrals as part of its marketing strategy?

20. What rationale is used for selecting marketing awareness tools?
21. Does the business use a contact management system?
22. What is the source of the business's market information, and how current is this data?
23. Who conducted the market analysis, and how valid is it today?
24. What is the public persona of the business?
25. Is the actual perception of the market consistent with the persona that marketing is trying to create?
26. Why did the customer choose this business over the competition?
27. Has the business conducted a recent competitive analysis?
28. Has the competitive analysis been verified externally, or does it reflect an unjustified bias toward the business?
29. How does the business establish a strategic plan for its products, and how well does it follow this plan?
30. Does the business follow a strategic plan that guides its future direction in the market?
31. How well does the strategic direction of the business align with the direction of the market?
32. How frequently does the business change its strategic plan?
33. Does the business have a person who is the visionary, and how has the visionary's participation in the business been secured for the future?
34. Does the business have a formalized process for collecting customer feedback as part of its product management?
35. What industry working groups, conference committees, or standards groups does the business participate in to remain current with the market?
36. Does the business follow a defined sales process?
37. Can the business explain its sales model and defend the rationale behind it?
38. Has the efficiency of the sales process improved over time?
39. How does the business monitor and measure its sales pipeline results?
40. What is the conversion ratio from leads to prospects and from prospects to customers? Is there statistical significance in the accuracy of these numbers?

41. Does the business focus on managing individual leads, or does it make decisions based on feedback from sales metrics?
42. Is there a list of current and past customers?
43. Are the sales projections based on the closure of sales to specific customers, or do they reflect an effective long-term strategy?
44. How does the business qualify its sales leads to validate them as sales prospects?
45. Are there any plans to change sales territories?
46. How does the business manage its sales territories and allocate the sales representatives' rights to mine these territories?
47. How does the business qualify its channel partners?
48. What type of training and support does the business provide for its channel partners?

CHAPTER 8

Assessment of the Organizational Infrastructure

In 1876 Army Major Henry Robert was asked to lead a public meeting at his local church. Conducting public meetings was not an activity the major was accustomed to, and he approached the task with some trepidation. He was no doubt used to military order and discipline, and he wasn't prepared for the chaos that went with public meetings. People spoke when they felt like it, and they listened when they felt like it. The major felt that holding open public meetings was a highly inefficient way to accomplish anything. He struggled through his meeting, but he told people later that he had fully lost control and, in the end, hadn't accomplished any of his goals.

As his military career advanced, the major continued to travel extensively throughout the United States working with local governments and the public, and his need to speak at public events continued. As he traveled, he also found that different geographic regions of the country followed different customs when conducting meetings, and this just added more confusion when working with different groups of people. There was no structure or rule to govern how people interacted, and public gatherings were so unproductive that he believed they were a waste of time. Most people of his day felt that real work was accomplished only behind closed doors, but this wasn't a very good image for the major's meetings that were supposed to be open to the general public. To solve his problem, Major Robert published the first edition of *Robert's Rules of Order*. These rules were based loosely on parliamentary law and, when followed, added both structure and process to public meetings. Because the use of *Robert's Rules of Order* (www.robertsrules.com) meant it was possible to achieve meaningful results, they continue to be used and are published in their tenth edition today.

All businesses are different, and there are no standards like the *Robert's Rules of Order* to guide their operations. Time and planning are

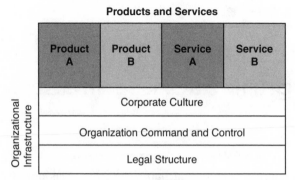

Figure 8.1 The Infrastructure Layers

required to define the organizational infrastructure that allows a business to efficiently accomplish its goals.

The organizational infrastructure of the business consists of three layers (see Figure 8.1), which are used to develop and support all of the products the business sells. Each infrastructure layer can be defined with increasing levels of formality. The first layer of the organization is defined by the declaration of the business's legal structure (corporation, partnership, C corporation, S corporation, and so on). This layer is the formal legal structure of the organization, and it is defined when the business is chartered. The middle layer of the organizational infrastructure is less formal, and it is defined by the command and control structure of the business (its organization chart). The final layer has the least formality. It is defined by the corporate culture that establishes the business's working environment and public persona.

The formal and informal layers of the organizational infrastructure vary greatly from one business to another. The legal structure of a business may be a limited liability corporation (LLC) or a C corporation, but the business may also operate with a very casual and relaxed culture or it might have a very strict or very formal culture. The combined formal and informal organizational structures are used to support and control the way the business operates. The organizational infrastructure is the foundation of the business, and it is designed to support the development and sale of the business's products and services.

Since the structure of a business can take many forms, within *Operations Due Diligence* I have attempted to avoid any implication that one structure is better or less risky than another. Only broad functional generalizations of departments have been used when describing functions of a business, and I have tried to avoid referring to any specific organizational structures whenever possible.

The organizational infrastructure must be able to support the current operations, and it must be capable of scaling along with the business as it grows. In many cases, the organizational infrastructure has evolved organically and has grown overly complex as a result of historic corporate events and past decisions rather than being implemented by design. The structure has evolved from personal relationships, acquisitions, promises made, and other events that were not implemented with the goal of optimizing the business based on its long-term operational needs alone. *Has the structure of the business been optimized according to its planned growth, or does it reflect organic growth?*

COMMAND AND CONTROL STRUCTURE

Defining the command and control structure means identifying the operating departments and making decisions about the chain of command. More important, creating an organization chart requires making decisions about the delegation of authority to individuals (and eventually holding those individuals accountable for their job performance). Publishing an organization chart can be one of the more painful exercises some businesses go through, and it often results in bruised egos and feigned surprise. "You mean I now work for her!" "That's not what I understood." It's almost as if some businesses would rather live with their inefficiencies than make the tough decisions required to publish their organization chart. Businesses that operate in this manner avoid formalizing their command and control structure and choose to accept the operational inefficiencies instead. *Does the business have a published organization chart, and are the employees aware of it?*

Without a defined command and control structure, there is a constant risk of operations inefficiency that results from the time spent determining "who does what" each time a new project comes along. Tasks are not performed because no one has been specifically assigned responsibility for them. "I thought it was someone else's job to do that." Some businesses just don't seem to be able to get out of their own way in this regard, and every new task becomes a new adventure. *Does the structure of the business support the use of repeatable processes, or is each new project a one-of-a-kind solution?*

Job Descriptions

Military organizations have rigid hierarchical structures based on clear lines of authority and responsibility. Without this, military organizations would not have the discipline they need to succeed. While most of us don't want to work in an environment as strict as a military organization, there is a clear necessity to define the role, responsibilities, and standards for each person in an organization. The organization chart alone isn't sufficient to accomplish this. It simply defines the framework of the organization. The title "vice president," for example, has different meanings in different businesses. Aside from knowing what their position is in the hierarchy of the business, a job description defines the employees' role, declares what their responsibilities are, sets the standards for their job, and lists the authority that has been allocated to them to accomplish their job. *Are the roles of each person in the organization clearly understood?*

Job descriptions are important for both the business and the employees alike. In order to hold employees accountable for their job performance, there needs to be a written description of their job and its performance requirements. A common practice is to ask employees to write their own job description, which the managers then review with the employees. This creates an opportunity for the managers to hold an open discussion about their expectations with the employees, and it sets the tone for future performance discussions between them. In many businesses, particularly large ones, there are generic job titles that are accompanied by broad job descriptions. These are important tools for large businesses because they help the businesses manage their labor grades, which in turn ensures fair treatment across a large number of employees. In these cases, it helps to accompany the broad job descriptions with a specific job description for each employee. *Does each employee have a written job description?*

Organization Charts

Military organizations follow another rule that all businesses would do well to adopt: authority can be delegated; responsibility cannot. This can also be stated this way: the responsibility for doing a job must be accompanied by the authority to accomplish it. Managers can delegate the authority to accomplish tasks to their staff, but the managers remain responsible for the performance of their staff. A manager who has authority to commit expenses up to $25,000 can delegate authority to his or her employees to spend within that amount, but if an employee spends more and the manager's budget is exceeded, the manager remains accountable for not having implemented tighter budget constraints or monitoring the staff more closely. Clear rules for the delegation of authority, along with the assignment of responsibilities, need to be established. *Does the business have defined lines of authority and responsibility?*

Authority can be delegated; responsibility cannot!

If we look at the organization chart as a command and control structure, it's easy to understand how problems can occur. (The topics of allocated legal and financial authorities are discussed further in Chapters 10 and 11.) The *hierarchical organization chart* (Figure 8.2) reflects the optimal command and control structure for a business. Management at the top of the hierarchy provides direction to the middle positions, which then control the

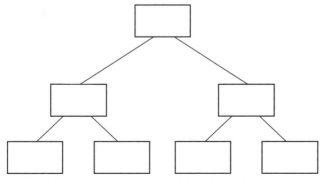

Figure 8.2 The Hierarchical Organization

lower-level functions of the organization. Most businesses are organized in this manner. While most businesses have a hierarchical organization chart, however, many don't operate according to their published structure.

The command and control structure of some businesses takes a form that is different from the hierarchy. The *person-centric organization* is an example of this. This type of command and control structure has obvious risks because of the over dependence on the person in the middle.

In the person-centric organization (Figure 8.3), one person becomes the spoke of a wheel with all others reporting only to him or her. All important decisions are held by this person, and nothing can happen without this person's direct action. It's easy to see how this structure occurs in a small business where the owner is an active participant in the business, but it's also seen in larger organizations when managers micromanage their staff. This occurs because the managers aren't able to trust their staff sufficiently to delegate authority to them. Obviously this indicates other potential problems including performance and trust issues, and identifying this type of structure can expose a significant operations risk. *Does the business have a hierarchical or a person-centric command and control structure?*

Another indicator of a person-centric organization can be found by looking at the span of control of the managers. If managers have too many direct employees and aren't able to effectively monitor their staff, than the managers' performance can begin to fall off. As a general rule,

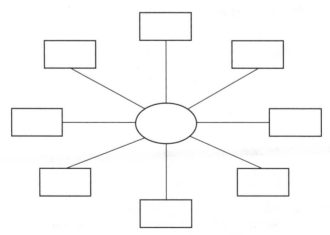

Figure 8.3 The Person-Centric Organization

8 to 10 employees is the top of the range, but this number is highly variable depending on the industry and business model being used. Delegating authority to the lower levels of the hierarchy is difficult for some managers because they resist releasing control to the lower levels of the organization by creating another level of middle managers or job supervisors. These managers just continue to pile more direct reports on themselves until they are so overworked that they can't effectively manage. *How many direct reports are controlled by each manager?*

Dotted-line organizations (Figure 8.4) are attempts to create hybrid relationships within the organizational structure. In a dotted-line organization, the published organizational structure shows an employee reporting to one manager when he or she is actually taking direction from another. The command and control structure of these businesses has been intentionally corrupted. Dotted-line organizations often reflect the reality of the way a business operates, but they are rarely documented.

In a dotted-line organization, it can eventually become impossible to determine who is really in control. "My supervisor asked me to do that, but his manager told me to do this instead." These structures are often the result of temporary or short-term staffing changes that remain in place over time.

Dotted-line organizations can be a source of tremendous employee frustration and can become disruptive to the operation of the entire business. Temporary assignments that result in dotted-line relationships should be identified as temporary and removed once the need for the temporary change is over. The business needs to be able to work within a defined

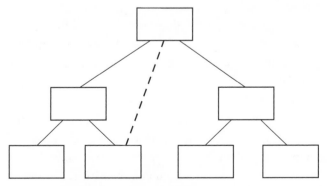

Figure 8.4 The Dotted-Line Organization

command and control structure, and dotted-line relationships that operate outside the organization are potential risks. *Is there a dotted-line organization in place that encourages working outside the published organizational structure? If so, why is this necessary?*

Creating an effective employee team is a long and arduous task. When deciding how to place employees in an organization, managers must consider the individual skills of each employee and determine how to use each individual as a team resource. Organizations are put together like jigsaw puzzles, and fitting the skills of each employee into a successful team takes time. It means understanding the strengths and weaknesses of individual employees and determining how best to utilize their skills. Since skill levels differ greatly from one employee to another, no two organizations are likely to be structured the same way to accomplish similar goals.

The organizational structure may also need to be adjusted as employees change. If the employees are in fact "the business's most valuable asset," as businesses commonly claim (and you can determine that the BS Quotient is low when this claim is made), then some of the most difficult work required to build a new organization may have already been accomplished, which offers a great platform to further grow the business. *Do the employees have all of the needed skills for the business to succeed?*

Management, Management, Management

Many investors say they look for three things when assessing a business: "Management, management, management." Identifying the risks and opportunities that exist within the management team can be difficult. Your goal is to assess the combined strength of the management team. Individual managers contribute their individual skills and experience as an element of the management team, and it is the combined strength (or weakness) of the team that causes the business to operate successfully (or unsuccessfully).

The management team should be assessed by examining its skills in each of the operations infrastructure areas. In order to assess the combined skills of the team, you will need to create a *management team skills matrix*. This is done by listing the eight infrastructure areas and rating the relative skills of each member of the management team for each of the areas. The management titles listed on the matrix in Figure 8.5 are only examples.

	CEO	President	CFO	CTO	Sales Manager	Support Manager		Highest Team Skill
Customer Satisfaction Infrastructure	5	2	0	2	4	7		7
Production Infrastructure	4	3	0	7	3	4		7
Information Management Infrastructure	1	7	3	5	3	4		7
Sales and Marketing Infrastructure	4	4	4	2	8	5		8
Organizational Infrastructure	8	4	1	5	2	0		8
Personnel Infrastructure	1	1	2	0	2	2		2
Financial Infrastructure	2	3	3	1	1	1		3
Legal Infrastructure	7	4	4	2	1	1		7

0 = No Skills   5 = Average Skills   10 = Advanced Skills

Figure 8.5 A Management Team Skills Matrix

You will need to identify who the members of the management team are. The skills rating must be appropriate to the needs of the business. A chief financial officer (CFO), for instance, may be highly skilled when running a $10 million organization but those skills may not be sufficient if the organization grows to $50 million. By assessing the management team in this manner, you will also gain further insight into the operations of the business. *Who are the members of the management team?*

Management team skill ratings are made by assessing the team's skills in each of the infrastructure areas (Figure 8.5). When a team member is proficient in an infrastructure area and meets all requirements, it would be rated as a 5 (the standard is a bell curve). Specific rationale should be used to justify higher or lower ratings. This method is intended to look at the entire management team and is not used for individual performance assessments (that is a separate activity). If you use this method to rate individuals, you may not get a proper rating for the business.

The marketing manager may be an excellent employee and have great marketing skills but would not be expected to possess all of the skills needed to operate the business. This method also works well as a self-assessment exercise for the management team. After constructing the skills matrix, you will use this information to construct a *management team skills arachnid* (Figure 8.6) by identifying where the highest team skill falls in each area.

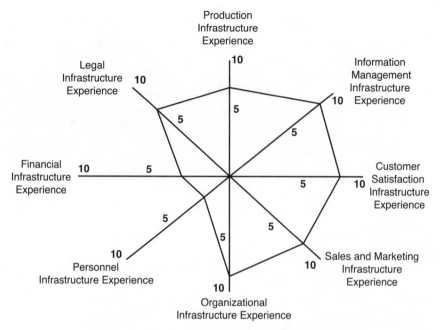

Figure 8.6 A Management Team Skills Arachnid

In the example arachnid, the business clearly has a risk in financial and personnel management. This might indicate that an investor will need to consider replacing or supplementing the CFO. There also appears to be an overall low ranking in personnel infrastructure experience. This could be a tremendous risk indicator, and it may need to be mitigated through management team training sessions or more severe steps. *Is there a management team skills matrix?*

CORPORATE CULTURE

The corporate culture of a business is established by the policies and standards that the business enforces for its employees, by the type and volume of work the employees are expected to produce and by the working environment the business creates. While the corporate culture is the least formal layer of the organizational infrastructure, establishing the correct corporate culture is as important to the success of a business as establishing the correct legal structure. Time, effort, and forethought need to be committed to the design of the corporate culture.

Businesses develop a reputation for their corporate culture. They become known for their working conditions and for the attitude of their employees toward one another. The corporate culture of the business is often a factor in attracting new employees. "I wouldn't work for that sweat shop." The corporate culture is also quite different from the public persona marketing creates for the business. The public facing persona of a business may be highly professional and formal while the corporate culture remains very casual and relaxed. You will need to distinguish between these two during your assessment. *What is the corporate culture of the business?*

We tend to think of the corporate culture in terms of the level of formality the business expects from its employees. Employees are allowed to be casual, like wearing jeans in the office, or the business has established a more formal jacket-and-tie-only environment. While the dress code and formality of the business is an important consideration for the employees, there are more critical elements of the culture that need to be assessed. The manner in which employees interrelate with one another, their ethics when dealing with customers, or the way employees comply with operational requirements like safety standards are all cultural indicators. *What level of respect do employees show for one another including both professional respect and acceptance of diversity?*

If there is a culture of "get the deal no matter what the cost," there is a risk that the sales team will think it's OK to "bend the rules" when necessary. This risk is much greater if the corporate culture leads to a willingness to break the rules in activities like intellectual property infringement. *Does the corporate culture include a "make the deal at any cost" attitude?*

If safety standards are ignored or treated lightly by employees, it could be a great potential risk. "It's too hot to wear those hard hats. After the inspector leaves, we just throw them in the back of the truck." The employee attitude toward the standards the business has set is also a risk indicator. *What is the employee attitude toward compliance with safety standards?*

Businesses will generally clean up, dress up, and try to present a good image during a due diligence. You'll need to explore whether the business is presenting an image that is consistent with its actual day-to-day operations or whether it's putting on a show for the assessment team.

Watch for the BS Quotient to go up here! Your goal is to observe the true operations of the business. You can accomplish this by observing the interactions of the employees while you are on site.

If your due diligence is conducted in preparation for a potential merger or acquisition, you will need to determine if there is a potential culture clash between the new business's employees and the groups they will be merging into. If you are a bottom-line, "make the sale at any cost" type of individual and the sales team is accustomed to a much more laid-back approach, then the business will likely not live up to your expectations, and the sales team may choose not to remain with the business for the long term. Likewise, if you follow high ethical standards and the management team is used to skirting the rules, the business could become a giant investment risk for you. An additional risk resulting from culture clash during a merger or acquisition occurs when employees form an attitude of "us versus them" with the new owners of the business. *Is there any risk of a future culture clash?*

The greatest risk of culture clash occurs in the highest levels of the organization. If the value system of the management team and your value system don't match, you would be wise to proceed with caution. A mismatch here could become a tremendous risk to the future operations of the business. *Do the values of the management team align with those of the investor?*

Culture Changes

It's very difficult to change the corporate culture once it's been established, and it's natural for employees to resist all culture changes. It's not unusual to experience some form of push back from employees when cultural changes are being made, regardless of the reasons for the change. Disrupting the established culture is always a risk. "We've done it this way for years. Why do we have to change just because we have new owners?" You can help mitigate this risk by allowing the employees to participate and influence the change process. Change initiatives, like most process improvement programs, work best when their membership is drawn from across the organization. It's easier to get employee buy-in when the employees contribute to the changes. *What is the employee attitude toward adopting culture changes?*

Adapting to change may not be as simple as requiring employees to follow a dress code. The corporate culture also includes the institutionalized processes and procedures of the business. Changing the culture often includes asking the employees to follow new procedures or workflows, effectively saying, "We want you to do the same job but to do it our way now." The institutionalized processes and procedures are the framework for the work environment that is used to "get things done."

When employees have become accustomed to their "old procedures" and feel ownership of them, they will resist changes, particularly if they participated in the creation of the original procedures. In these situations it may be important to explain that the previous processes weren't wrong or bad and the new company just does it differently and wants the employees to be part of the new team. If the new team has developed some advanced methods or intellectual property, this may also be an opportunity for the acquiring business to learn some new tricks by adopting the procedures of the new business. If the plan is to maintain the business in a separate facility and there are no driving reasons to make cultural changes, then the best risk mitigation might be not changing the culture and seriously considering the impact of any changes that are made. *Are the workflow and processes of the business based on any unique intellectual property?*

Managers who are using *Operations Due Diligence* as part of a self-assessment shouldn't discount the risk of cultural change either. As businesses grow, culture changes may be needed to support the growth. What is your strategy for making these necessary changes? *Are cultural changes anticipated for the business?*

Castle Cultures

Many businesses follow serial processes whereby one group does their part of the job and then passes it on to the next group to perform their job and so on down the line. These operations tend to form employees into isolated operational groups that are at risk of adopting a castle culture. In castle cultures, the employees in each group or department perform their own function and are responsible solely for the success of their own group. The scope of the group is limited to the responsibilities of their own immediate organization.

Eventually, when things go wrong, the groups start to blame one another for the failures, and this evolves into a culture in which each group becomes highly defensive, feeling they have to defend "their own turf" against that of others. They do this by putting up hypothetical walls (they create obstacles) to defend their own operations. "That's not our job." "We're not responsible for doing that." Each group is concerned only about their portion of the process and not for the success of the entire business. Many "e-mail wars" are fought by organizations with castle cultures as e-mails become the arrows shot over the walls of the castle! This type of operation is easily recognized because the employees have become highly defensive. When one group acts defensively, it puts the other groups on the defensive as well. Once a castle culture has been established, it becomes very difficult to correct it. *Are there any signs of castle culture behavior among the employees?*

The risks posed by castle cultures are mitigated by the use of cross-functional teams (also known as *integrated product teams*). Cross-functional teams are formed with members from across several groups, and they are given a shared goal. The team members are brought together for a single, highly focused mission that leverages their combined skills to solve a common problem, develop a product, or complete an assignment together. The use of this type of team approach stands out in contrast with the alternate, more traditional approach whereby "I do my job and hand it off for you to do your job." *Do the employees see themselves as members of a team?*

VIRTUAL ENVIRONMENTS

Technology has the ability to rapidly transform society. Technology, in the form of steam engines and the telegraph, launched the industrial revolution and transformed us from an agrarian into an urban society within a couple of decades. Likewise, personal computers, the availability of the high-speed Internet, and affordable cell phones have all affected the way we work today. When you add the additional disincentives of commuting to an office including commuting times, high gas prices, risks from man-made and natural disasters, child-care costs, and lifestyle constraints, there are plenty of reasons for employees to work remotely. When they do so, their jobs are considered to be *virtual jobs*.

Many jobs are now being performed virtually that would never have been considered for virtual jobs in the past. There is a growing tendency to ask why a job can't be done remotely rather than in the office. Why spend an hour commuting, only to sit in front of a computer, when you could use that time more productively by telecommuting? *Does the business allow telecommuting?*

Telecommuting has become an option for many employees, and more and more often it is also being acknowledged as an opportunity for the business. As society transitions toward the use of virtual work environments, we are also being forced to change the way we manage. There is no reason why software engineering and other highly computerized professions cannot be performed virtually if the employees are properly managed. Not having the overhead expenses of a large facility starts to make tremendous sense for businesses. This work situation can succeed if the business is prepared to manage a virtual team.

The greatest barrier to telecommuting may be educating old-school managers about new virtual management methods. A manager who needs to see the employee's fingers moving on the keyboard to verify that the employee is actually working represents a culture that has hopefully passed. We will find that virtual project management is one of the fastest-growing disciplines of the twenty-first century. Effective telecommuting requires managers to be trained in the management of virtual employees. *Has the management staff been trained in managing virtual employees?*

There are some jobs, such as manufacturing, that are the exceptions to this rule and cannot be performed from home. There are also people, such as parents with young children at home, who find that working in an office is their only option. Telecommuting is not an option for these employees, but for many others, telecommuting offers great benefits. The days of businesses housing all of their employees in tall office towers may well be behind us. Technology is the enabler for virtual employees. Virtual environments require remote access to the information management infrastructure, which means imposing strict controls on how these systems are used. The information management infrastructure must be designed to support virtual employees. This of course brings new risks that need to be understood and mitigated. *Have guidelines been established for virtual employees?*

The days of working in tall office buildings may well be behind us!

It's always a good idea for the business to provide the computers used by virtual employees rather than expecting the employees to use their personal computers. Because of the need to secure business data, plus the legal impact of business document retention policies, employees need to clearly separate business data from their personal data. There are exceptions to every rule, but this is one for which the risk to the business may be too great (unless the employees want to surrender the control over the content of their personal computers to the business). *How many employees are authorized to work virtually, how are they managed, and do they use personal equipment or equipment provided by the business?*

With the current state of technology, telecommuting may be to an employee's home across town or it could be to an offshore location 12,000 miles around the world. Telecommuting has enabled the use of remote employees in offshore locations. Managing offshore employees includes all of the risks of virtual management plus additional risks, such as intellectual property protection and international rules compliance, which must be mitigated. *Does the business use offshore employees?*

I recommend businesses establish the following minimum rules for virtual employees:

- Telecommuting must be presented to the employees as a privilege that must be continually earned.
- Before they can telecommute, employees must work in-house for a period of time so that they learn the business and so that the business can gauge their production capacity.
- Employees can and will be asked to work in-house at any time there is a need, and the employees must be available at these times as if they were in-house employees on a full-time basis.
- The business has the right to cancel this benefit, without cause, at any time.
- Since the business is allowing these employees to work from home, saving the employees commuting expenses, the business

is not responsible for employee-incurred expenses such as incidental telephone or Internet fees.

- A liability waiver must be signed by the employees.
- The virtual employees need to be available during a defined core work period.

ETHICS

A few years ago I accepted a position as chief operating officer (COO) for a small business that was owned and operated by a father and son team. I was a little apprehensive about taking a direct position with the business because I had been working as an independent consultant for quite a while. I went through the entire interview process before I finally met the father who was the CEO.

When I was introduced to the father, he asked me a couple of questions and eventually asked if there was anything I wanted to ask of them. I had only one question: "How honest are you guys?" I suspected that the question had caught him off guard. He thought about it for a couple of seconds and responded by saying he felt they were very honest. He also pointed out that there was a fallacy in my question. "If we were honest, I would say so. If we were not, I would still tell you we were honest." I explained that I understood this, but I wanted to go on record for the way I would operate their business. If I felt they were asking me to do something dishonest at any point, I would remind him of our conversation. I never had to remind them of our discussion, and I have had a great business relationship with the father and son, who are highly successful and I believe are proof that you can be honest and ethical and still succeed in business.

Not all business relationships work out this way. Sometimes it takes a while, but business is driven by relationships and reputations. I have no empirical data to point to, but I firmly believe that businesses that take the high road tend to succeed more often. At the point I find a business doesn't operate ethically, I drop it as a client and terminate the relationship. If you can't trust the people you work with to conduct business honorably and ethically, than you can expect that, at some point, they will treat you dishonorably and unethically. I am simply not willing to risk my reputation by working in an unethical environment. It's important to explore the record of the business and its officers to determine what their ethics culture is.

What is the demonstrated track record of the business in its hiring and promotion practices with regard to equal opportunity for its employees?

Sustainable businesses publish an ethics policy that they believe in and enforce. The ethics policy establishes the culture of the business, and it can help mitigate legal liability when employees violate the business's stated policy. *Does the business have a published ethics policy, and is each employee required to sign it?*

The risks associated with ethics violations can include civil and criminal penalties for individuals as well as for the business. Ethics policies typically address some or all of the subjects in the Ethics Policy Inclusions table. In today's litigious world, the ethics policy needs to clearly state the business's position on ethics issues, and the business needs to demonstrate its intention to aggressively enforce this policy.

The ethics policy should establish the business's policy with respect to sexual harassment of employees within the workplace. *How does the ethics policy address sexual harassment?*

Ethics Policy Inclusions

Sexual harassment	Employee relations
Equal opportunity	Director accountability
Product representations	Environmental impacts
Product quality	Government compliance
Sales dealings	Citizenship and community
International sales	

The ethics policy should establish the business's policy on equal employment opportunity. *How does the ethics policy address equal opportunity?*

The ethics policy should provide employees with guidance in the way they represent the product (such as product capabilities) when they are speaking with potential customers. *How does the ethics policy address product representations?*

Standards for product quality vary from business to business. Inexpensive products may not be built to the same quality standards as more expensive products, but the business should not misrepresent the quality of its products. The ethics policy should establish standards for the quality of products. *How does the ethics policy address product quality?*

Misrepresenting a product is only one potential ethics issue a business may face in its sales dealings. Other unethical practices such as kickbacks and bribes must be addressed by the ethics policy. *How does the ethics policy address sales dealings?*

The United States and many other countries have laws dealing with the way foreign sales may be conducted. Sales practices that are acceptable in one country may not be in another. Whenever a business is dealing with international sales, the ethics policy should establish standards for employee conduct in international sales. *How does the ethics policy address international sales?*

The ethics policy should establish standards for employee relations within the business. This includes mutual respect, public comments (such as social media postings), and other forms of behavior that could disrupt the business's operations. *How does the ethics policy address employee relations?*

The directors of the business have a unique responsibility to the shareholders, and the ethics policy should specifically define how they are expected to represent the business. *How does the ethics policy address director accountability?*

Businesses have not always been good neighbors. The ethics policy should define the environmental standards that will be used to guide the business. *How does the ethics policy address environmental impacts?*

Laws and government regulations are cost drivers for all businesses, and there is sometimes a temptation to cut corners. The ethics policy should provide guidance on government compliance. *How does the ethics policy address government compliance?*

A business is a citizen of the community in which it operates. Being a good citizen means participating in the life of the community through politics, charity, education, and many other areas. The ethics policy should establish guidelines for these activities. *How does the ethics policy address citizenship and community?*

Publishing an ethics policy alone is not sufficient. The first step in enforcement is to train all employees about the ethics rules of the business including the process for reporting violations. *Does the business require its employees to take ethics training?*

PHYSICAL SAFETY AND SECURITY

Providing physical safety and security to protect the employees and assets of the business is a necessity. The methods used to provide a safe secure environment against man-made and natural disasters have to be integrated seamlessly into the organizational infrastructure of the business with minimal intrusion into its operations. Deciding what actions need to be taken to create a secure environment has become much more complex than in the past, and determining what security measures to put in place requires careful prior planning and forethought.

Unfortunately, ensuring physical safety and security is no longer limited to fire drills as it was in the past, and real consideration needs to be given to other types of hazards such as biohazards as well as supporting the special needs of disabled employees. For a business whose products require the handling of hazardous materials, this plan is an absolute necessity. Sustainable businesses put a physical safety and security plan in place and give all employees training about their roles in advance. This training needs to include practice drills to ensure compliance. Emergency drills for all employees also need to include evacuation procedures for employees with special needs. *Is there a safety and security plan in place? Has the business complied with the Americans with Disabilities Act, and how has this been reflected in its hiring and promotion practices?*

Physical safety and security procedures need to cover all of the potential hazards an employee is likely to face. Such procedures include, but are not limited to, providing controlled security entrances, toxic substance labeling, and warnings on hazardous equipment and facilities, as well as removing asbestos dust in older buildings. The physical safety and security procedures must also address the needs of employees with special needs. I have hired numerous employees with special needs, including one of the best software engineers I have ever worked with who was a quadriplegic. He used a mouth stick to write code and performed above average for the team. His greatest fear was fires. The software group worked on the second floor of an older facility. Our procedures were modified to add a safe room that he could go to in case of fire, and we assigned a team to be there to help him including carrying him from the facility if need be. This routine was practiced in each of our fire drills. *Does the business conduct a periodic analysis of the safety and security risks for both the assets and the employees, including those with special needs, to ensure that there is a safe work environment?*

Summary of the Organizational Infrastructure Questions

1. Has the structure of the business been optimized according to its planned growth, or does it reflect organic growth?
2. Does the business have a published organization chart, and are the employees aware of it?
3. Does the structure of the business support the use of repeatable processes, or is each new project a one-of-a-kind solution?
4. Are the roles of each person in the organization clearly understood?
5. Does each employee have a written job description?
6. Does the business have defined lines of authority and responsibility?
7. Does the business have a hierarchical or a person-centric command and control structure?
8. How many direct reports are controlled by each manager?
9. Is there a dotted-line organization in place that encourages working outside the published organizational structure? If so, why is this necessary?
10. Do the employees have all of the needed skills for the business to succeed?
11. Who are the members of the management team?
12. Is there a management team skills matrix?
13. What is the corporate culture of the business?
14. What level of respect do employees show for one another including both professional respect and acceptance of diversity?
15. Does the corporate culture include a "make the deal at any cost" attitude?
16. What is the employee attitude toward compliance with safety standards?
17. Is there any risk of a future culture clash?
18. Do the values of the management team align with those of the investor?
19. What is the employee attitude toward adopting culture changes?

20. Are the workflow and processes of the business based on any unique intellectual property?
21. Are cultural changes anticipated for the business?
22. Are there any signs of castle culture behavior among the employees?
23. Do the employees see themselves as members of a team?
24. Does the business allow telecommuting?
25. Has the management staff been trained in managing virtual employees?
26. Have guidelines been established for virtual employees?
27. How many employees are authorized to work virtually, how are they managed, and do they use personal equipment or equipment provided by the business?
28. Does the business use offshore employees?
29. What is the demonstrated track record of the business in its hiring and promotion practices with regard to equal opportunity for its employees?
30. Does the business have a published ethics policy, and is each employee required to sign it?
31. How does the ethics policy address sexual harassment?
32. How does the ethics policy address equal opportunity?
33. How does the ethics policy address product representations?
34. How does the ethics policy address product quality?
35. How does the ethics policy address sales dealings?
36. How does the ethics policy address international sales?
37. How does the ethics policy address employee relations?
38. How does the ethics policy address director accountability?
39. How does the ethics policy address environmental impacts?
40. How does the ethics policy address government compliance?
41. How does the ethics policy address citizenship and community?
42. Does the business require its employees to take ethics training?
43. Is there a safety and security plan in place?
44. Has the business complied with the Americans with Disabilities Act, and how has this been reflected in its hiring and promotion practices?
45. Does the business conduct a periodic analysis of the safety and security risks for both the assets and the employees, including those with special needs, to ensure that there is a safe work environment?

CHAPTER 9

Assessment of the Personnel Infrastructure

In the mid-nineteenth century, the Endicott-Johnson Corporation (EJ) became the model for benevolent businesses. EJ was an employee-centric business that manufactured shoes in the boom of the industrial revolution. EJ's use of evolving technology (by nineteenth-century standards) and automation of its factories revolutionized both the methods used for manufacturing shoes and the lifestyle of its workforce.

EJ was a paternalistic business formed by Horace N. Lester,* and it was originally known as the Lester Boot and Shoe Company. Lester built his business following what became known as the Lester Plan. The Lester Plan included the development of Lester-Shire, which was a company-planned community created to entice people to move out of the surrounding rural areas and go to work for Lester's growing business. Lester developed his town by either leasing or mortgaging the real estate to his employees. In an era when transportation was difficult, Lester-Shire offered rural families an incentive to locate near work, and the company offered many other benefits, including affordable housing and lower prices at the company store. Lester-Shire became known for its many parks and carousels (many of which still operate today), and it helped Lester attract workers to its factories. For the Lester Company, this meant it had the ability to hire less expensive, unskilled labor to work on its assembly lines rather than having to depend on the craftspeople traditionally used to make shoes. This made great sense for investors as well, including Henry B. Endicott who recognized the economic advantages the Lester Plan offered and who later took control of the Lester Company.

---

*The information in this section was graciously contributed with permission from the dissertation of Professor Gerald Zahavi, Department of History, State University of New York at Albany (www.albany.edu/history/ej/origins/).

As the Endicott-Johnson Corporation grew through a public offering and several mergers, EJ eventually became one of the largest shoe manufacturers in the world. The need for boots to support the Civil War accelerated EJ's growth. EJ continued the Lester Plan of being benevolent and paternalistic to its employees, and it became world renowned for doing so. Since many of the employees had recently immigrated to the United States, word quickly spread back to the old country, and Endicott-Johnson became famous as new immigrants came off the boat with their only English being to recite the saying "which way EJ."

It's easy to understand why the EJ employees were loyal and motivated, but there was also a dark side to this type of paternalism. If the business dismissed employees for some reason, it could mean the immediate loss of the home they rented, or it could mean the foreclosure on their company-sponsored mortgage. It could also mean the immediate closing of their account at the company store. Furthermore, if employees bought a house outside of Lester-Shire, they could lose their job for doing so. These policies were a great way for EJ to ensure employee loyalty and workforce stability, even though they limited the employees' options. Employees accepted these terms when they joined the EJ company. *What is the longevity and average turnover rate of employees?*

The personnel infrastructure is the system of compensation, benefits, and human resources services that form the framework a business uses to manage its employees. This is the framework that assures the business that it has the correct employees and it employs them at an affordable price to perform the work of the business.

Each employee is a human asset of the business. When assessing the other parts of the organizational infrastructure, you have been exploring the roles and responsibilities of each staff position. You have performed this assessment as an exploration of the structure of the business. During the personnel assessment, you are exploring the support systems for the business's human assets (what should each asset cost, what steps the business has taken to protect and maintain its human assets, and the way these methods are used to sustain the business).

While the business is staffed by individuals, it has a legal persona of its own. The framework provided by the personnel infrastructure forms the bridge between the business persona and the people who are employed by the business. The organizational infrastructure deals with what employees are doing while the personnel infrastructure deals with why they are doing it.

> The organizational infrastructure deals with what employees are doing while the personnel infrastructure deals with why they are doing it.

EMPLOYEE BENEFITS

Benevolence today comes primarily in the form of employee benefits. This benevolence is offered because the labor market drives the business to compete for skilled employees rather than being the result of any paternalism toward the employees (however, there are some true exceptions to this).

There are many factors that impact the desire of employees to work for a business, and these vary greatly depending on the personal needs and motivation of each employee. A benefit for one employee may not be seen as a benefit to another. Benefits drive the overhead costs of the business, and therefore there is a trade-off between costs and benefits that has to be balanced. Benefits are drivers of employee risk and opportunity in the form of employee motivation, loyalty, and other areas that are difficult to measure but which, in the end, help to determine the competitiveness of the business in the labor market. The benefit package the business offers is driven by competitive pressure from the labor market and, in some cases, through formal negotiations such as organized labor agreements. This is also an area where government regulations regarding benefits, such as health care, have become cost drivers, and it is important to understand the impact of these benefits based on the projected growth of the business. *What government regulations affect the employee benefit packages today and in the foreseeable future?*

In 2010 the U.S. federal government implemented the Patient Protection and Affordable Care Act. In 2011 the U.S. Congress started action to replace this legislation. Many of the claims being made about this legislation, both for and against, were based on arguments about the financial impact of the legislation on businesses. One thing is certain, however: there are and will continue to be many government regulations that impact the benefits businesses offer to their employees. These regulations impact health care, pensions, safety, and almost every other area of an organization. Further, these regulations are greatly affected by economics and political change at every level of government. All businesses must have a plan to proactively monitor and adjust to these changes within their legal, financial, and operations infrastructures. *How does the business proactively monitor changing regulations that could impact its legal, financial, and operations infrastructure?*

There are many businesses, particularly small businesses, that genuinely want to help their employees. There are also businesses that see their employees as fully replaceable, and they offer only the bare minimum benefits necessary to attract the talent they need. Common benefits include 401(k) contributions, health-care plans, tuition reimbursement plans, paid time off, and similar types of traditional benefit programs that are either fully or partially paid for by the business plus pure compensation-based items such as options plans and bonuses. *Does the business publish a list of employee benefits?*

As with culture changes, changes to the employee benefit plans may not be easily accepted by the employees. In cases where the business is experiencing a merger or acquisition, and where a combination or revision of the employee benefits will likely occur, care must be taken. If the announcement of benefit changes is the first exposure the employees have to the new organization, it can become the source for rejection of the new organization that will be difficult to overcome. The risk from changing benefits is one of the greatest causes of employee dissatisfaction during M&A events. Many times as a business grows, the benefits improve; these improvements can be presented to the employees in a positive manner and leveraged as an opportunity to improve employee morale. *Are there any anticipated changes in the employee benefit plan?*

Employers can also offer *fringe benefits*—that is, benefits that cost money for the company but that do not affect wage rates. Examples of fringe benefits are on-site child care, automobile allowances, cell phone usage, Internet fee reimbursement, tuition reimbursement, paid club and gym dues, salary continuance for military or jury duty, or social events and clubs. These and other fringe benefits add to the company's overhead, but they also raise employee morale. A business's fringe benefits may offer a large cost payback advantage because the cost to the business of the fringe benefits is generally low but the benefits are seen as highly valuable by the employees. *What fringe benefits does the business offer its employees?*

Removing a benefit is a risk because of the wide variance in the way employees may value the benefit. Any benefit changes can quickly become an emotional discussion with an employee. The cost of a benefit doesn't always align with the importance an employee places on the benefit. The business may be able to leverage less expensive benefits into greater levels of employee satisfaction through careful planning. To do this, it is important to recognize that a benefit to one employee, such as on-site child care, might not be seen as a benefit by employees without young children. Even benefits such as a health-care plan that may be highly valued by some employees might have no value for employees that have coverage through a spouse or parent. *Does the business conduct an annual benefits review and planning session?*

EMPLOYEE COMPENSATION

Employee compensation includes the employees' base salaries plus any other financial incentives including commissions; bonuses; company contributions to health, life, and professional insurance; 401(k) contributions; educational reimbursements; stocks and options; plus fringe benefits such as vehicle, telephone, Internet, office and furnishings, housing and support service allowances, club dues, and any other items that the employees are recompensed for in return for their services.

I am including all of the employees' perceived benefits as well as the actual compensation employees receive from the business (which may not be consistent with the IRS's definition of *compensation*). All forms of compensation need to be planned and budgeted by the business. If the business gives an average 5 percent annual salary increase to all employees, this inflation needs to be reflected in the budget (and if this was previously given but will no longer be "standard" in the future, it should be identified as a potential risk). *Is the annual growth in employee compensation planned, and has it been budgeted?*

If there are allowances paid that the employees benefit from (for example, car allowances), then the employees will consider these as part of their compensation. In this case, the employees perceive the automobile allowance as a benefit because they have the use of an automobile. *What compensation packages do employees currently receive including both salary and benefits?*

Employee compensation is based on the job being performed by the individual (unless the job is subject to collective bargaining), and an annual compensation plan needs to be created that establishes the parameters for all employee compensation. *Are employee salaries subject to collective bargaining?*

If compensation hasn't been established in a fair, consistent manner for all employees, then this is a potential risk. As part of the Operations Due Diligence, you will need to request a list by element (salary, bonus, options, and so on) of any compensation provided for each employee for the last three years and a list of all scheduled or promised future compensation. Some businesses provide individual compensation reports to each employee, listing all of the elements and cost of the employee's compensation including both the employee and the business contribution toward these benefits. Once employees consider an item as part of their compensation, it will be difficult to remove the item since the employees will see it as reducing their compensation. Once established therefore, these costs become recurring expenses for the business. You need to explore what the real cost for all employee compensation is and determine what compensation promises or understandings have been made that might not have been documented. *How does the business track all of the elements of its employees' compensation?*

Assessing the methods used to establish employee compensation, including the value of all benefit packages included in the employee compensation plans, may indicate additional cost risks or opportunities. There are many online resources available for researching industry average salaries. Some of the more popular sites are notoriously biased either toward the business or toward the employees. Multiple inputs need to be used to support this analysis, with care being used to determine regional differences. *Does the business analyze the competitive salary range for each position or conduct a periodic review of the cost of benefits to ensure that its compensation rates are competitive? How does the business establish the salary and benefit guidelines for the next year?*

You will need to explore whether there were any undocumented compensation promises or understandings made with any employees. It's not uncommon to hear that a key employee is leaving a company because the new management did not give him or her a promotion that was previously promised and was never included in the budget. Documented increases, such as key employee contracts and cost-of-living increases also need to be reflected in future budgets and plans. *Have all promised compensation increases been documented and included in the compensation plan?*

THE BUSINESS-EMPLOYEE RELATIONSHIP

As part of your Operations Due Diligence, you will need to request a list of all full-time, part-time, and contract employees currently employed by the business or employed by the business within the past three years. If you are short on time, then the personnel infrastructure is a good place to focus your efforts. The personnel infrastructure is a target rich area that can offer more insight into the operation of the business than any other area, but exploring these relationships can be difficult.

When it comes to their employees, businesses run the full range from benevolence to belligerence, and employees tend to respond in kind. The interaction of employees with the business can make or break it. The true relationship between employees and the business (and other employees) isn't usually acknowledged publicly. "I'm just here to collect my paycheck. Don't ask me to do anything extra." "These guys have taken good care of me." "I'll do anything to help them." Sentiments like these can run as an undercurrent that can move and change the direction of the business before problems are recognized.

Some businesses end up in a game of tug-of-war, with their employees pulling on one end of the rope and management pulling on the opposite end (see Figure 9.1). You will need to explore the working relationship between the business and its employees to discover any risk of any disruptive employee relationships. Management can also be the source of disruptive relationship

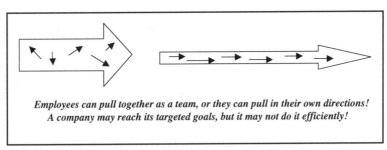

Employees can pull together as a team, or they can pull in their own directions!
A company may reach its targeted goals, but it may not do it efficiently!

Figure 9.1 Employees Should Align as One Team

risks. This is sometimes seen when managers view themselves as coaches rather than as contributing team members and they "watch the action from the sidelines," holding the employees responsible rather than stepping in like a quarterback calling the game from the thick of the action. *What is the working relationship between the employees and the business?*

Organized labor places a third party in the middle of the business-employee relationship. You will need to explore any potential role that organized labor plays in the business-employee relationship. It's absolutely critical that you understand the nature of any current organized labor agreements or any that are being discussed with the business. *Are there any existing agreements with organized labor? Are there any known or ongoing actions to organize employees within the business?*

FAIR EMPLOYMENT PRACTICES

Treating all employees and potential employees equally, fairly, and with respect is good business. In a modern society, there is no place for unfair or unethical employment practices. Unfair or unethical employment practices are bad for business. It's that simple.

And yet, some businesses continue to run into problems with their employment practices. This is certainly true if you consider the volume of litigation resulting from violations of the employment practice laws that occur annually.

> Treating all employees and potential employees equally, fairly, and with respect is good business. It's that simple.

For every case in which a business is found guilty of violating employment laws, there are many cases where the business was truly not at fault but ends up paying for an expensive defense against false accusations. These accusations come from former employees hoping to benefit from a quick settlement with a business that wants to avoid having its name tied to this type of charge in a public courtroom. We live in a litigious world. It seems the more success a business has, the more likely it is that individuals seeking fast cash will bring about some form of litigation, which can result in high fines and lost reputation. Sustainable businesses establish a strategy for protecting themselves against fraudulent employment claims while ensuring that their employment practices are absolutely sound. *Does the business review its employment practices on an annual basis?*

Avoiding litigation, controlling labor costs, finding the talent and skills to keep a business competitive, and dealing with a wide range of human emotions are all stresses placed on the personnel infrastructure. These stresses alone should be enough to force discipline into any business. Risks to the personnel infrastructure need to be mitigated on a continuing basis. All personnel actions, particularly those pertaining to hiring and terminating employees, need to be guided by the recurring use of a formalized process. *Are there established processes for hiring and terminating employees?*

HIRING, FIRING, AND EVERYTHING IN BETWEEN

Defined processes need to be in place for all recurring employment actions and should be followed rigorously for all personnel actions without exception. Many businesses follow a two-person rule and ensure that all personnel actions related to hiring or firing be attended by two people when meeting with the employee. For contentious personnel actions, one of the participants is typically a trained specialist such as another experienced manager or an HR representative. In all cases, notes need to be taken and saved in the employee personnel files. Problems occur when there are exceptions made to the rules, so getting the rules right and then sticking to them is the best way to mitigate these risks. *Are personnel actions and discussions documented in the employee personnel files?*

The Hiring Process

The business should have a staffing policy to guide the hiring of all new employees. The hiring process starts with a written job description that defines the standards for the position. The standards include the experience, education, and past accomplishments that are required to qualify candidates for the position.

The type of position—professional, technical, or something else— determines the approach to be used for recruiting and the search requirements, such as how far the candidate search will extend geographically. Some businesses prefer to conduct their employment searches internally, and others prefer to go through staffing recruiters. This is strictly a preference of the business and will vary depending on the type of position and the anticipated difficulty identifying and processing qualified candidates. Businesses often use online automated databases to collect applications and résumés. These databases allow easy searches for qualified candidates from large numbers of applicants. In a labor market where the business anticipates receiving hundreds (or thousands) of résumés in response to an advertisement, the recruiter provides the temporary labor needed to vet a large number of applications. The recruiter qualifies the candidates and creates a short list, which saves management time. *Does the business follow a documented staffing policy?*

Sign-on bonuses and relocation packages are offered for some positions. Hiring incentives such as these often have contingency requirements, such as *time-in-service*, which requires the employee to remain in the job for some period to earn the bonus. This type of nonrecurring compensation can represent a significant risk if there are hidden costs that you are not aware of and which can be easily overlooked in future budgets. *Are there any outstanding employee sign-on incentives? If so, what is their value, and when do they mature?*

Once a short list of potential candidates has been created, the interview process begins. Many businesses have become creative in the way they conduct interviews. Telephone interviews are used to narrow down the candidate list further (plus save on travel costs). Power interviews and peer interviews, where candidates are interviewed by groups of people, have also become popular because they put the candidates in stressful or realistic job situations and allow the group to interact with them in near realistic environments. It's important that all of the participants in the hiring process receive instruction in how to conduct an interview and what their role is in the interview. Participants must also be instructed to treat the candidates with respect and to respect the absolute need for confidentiality regarding the candidates' records, even including the fact that the candidate is interviewing. *Is training required for all employees who are involved in the recruiting process?*

There are specialized services available for conducting candidate background searches. In many cases a simple Internet search can be revealing. It's important, however, to remember that, while there is a lot of data available on the Internet, this information is totally uncontrolled and may not be accurate. Candidates can be asked about information found during this search; however, because so much personal information can end up online, these questions need to be approached carefully and strictly limited to the candidates' professional activities. *Are background searches conducted for all employment candidates?*

One of my standard interview questions is to ask candidates what they found out about the business or its products from reviewing our website. Surprisingly, I still get candidates who say they haven't looked at the site. In my mind, these candidates have failed to do their basic homework, and it automatically disqualifies them. For those who have done their homework, this is a great benchmarking question telling me about the candidates' basic drives and abilities.

A good time to start a candidate's personnel file is with the candidate's completed standardized application form, which has usually been completed prior to the interview. Employment forms need to be retained whether a candidate is hired or not. If a person is interviewed and not hired, that person's file is a good place to document the reasons for not hiring him or her. *Are all applicants required to fill out a standardized application form?*

Once a decision has been made to hire particular candidates, an employment offer letter is written that documents the employment offer. Employment offer letters outline the full compensation package the candidates will receive, plus any terms and conditions of their employment, the start date, and the direct manager they will be reporting to. Offer letters should be sent from HR or whoever has the centralized control over all hiring activities for the business. Generally, functional managers don't send the offer letter because there is a risk of compliance violations from managers who have not been properly trained and there is also a risk of the business losing staffing control. The offer letter must be dated and state how long the offer is valid for. The format the business uses for employment letters should be reviewed by an attorney. *Is there a single point of control for all staffing decisions?*

It's never a good idea to withdraw an offer letter after it has been sent to a candidate unless a contingency has been specifically stated in the offer (such as an offer contingent on a background search). It is unconscionable to me that any business would put itself at risk by rescinding an offer letter . . . and yet, I have seen it happen twice. In one case, the manager sent an offer letter to a candidate and then found out that a more qualified candidate was available. He then rescinded the original offer letter, after the candidate had already resigned his current job. In the second instance, an offer letter was sent; the candidate accepted the new position and resigned from his current job. When the CEO he had been working for received the resignation, he called the CEO from the new company, and a deal was made between the two CEOs, at which point the offer letter was rescinded. Imagine the position these employees were put in and the risk the businesses put themselves in. I consider this unethical and a serious risk on the part of the business. *Does the business have a policy controlling employment offers?*

Performance Appraisals

Appraisals formalize frank discussions between employees and their managers regarding the employees' job performance. The appraisal process forces managers and their employees to discuss their expectations for the job and allows the managers to state how well the employees are performing. It also forces the managers to logically consider the value of the employees' work and to establish performance standards for the job. *Is there an established process for conducting employee performance appraisals?*

It's good to be the boss. Everyone likes to give good performance appraisals and tell the employees what a great job they've done and then reward them with a big raise. Unfortunately, performance appraisals don't all go that way, and that's when being the boss becomes stressful. "You failed to meet your goals this year, and you are therefore receiving a low raise" can be a tough message to deliver. What about situations in which the message is "You have been doing a great job, but the business just isn't able to give any raises this year"? *Are performance appraisals tied to increases in salary and/or bonuses, and how has the business planned for these increases?*

Most managers have never been trained to give effective performance appraisals and don't know how to give a negative appraisal or the importance of doing so when it is justified. The managers' job is to hire, direct, lead, and support their employees, enabling them to meet the standards set for their job. If managers aren't willing or don't have the skills to tell employees that they're not performing, then the managers are failing to do their own jobs. What I find is that many managers learn to write and conduct performance appraisals as on-the-job training, gained mostly through receiving their own reviews, but they have never received formalized training in this important skill. *Are managers trained to conduct effective performance appraisals?*

Employee performance can change, improving or degrading over time. The result is inconsistent performance from year to year. In some years employees are highly productive, and in others the same employees can perform poorly. Employee goals may change from year to year (the bar may be placed higher or lower), and other personal and professional events can cause fluctuations in their performance including health, family status, education, and their ability to evolve along with their job. Most businesses recognize this and take a long-term view when assessing the value of their employees. This is why businesses offer support services when employees run into personal or professional problems such as substance abuse or family counseling, because they believe that in the long run, investing in their existing employees is better than finding, hiring, and training new ones. *Does the business have performance appraisals for each employee for the preceding three years?*

Promotions

Promoting employees from within offers some real advantages for a business (and some risk). One obvious advantage is the motivation a promotion brings. Employees who anticipate promotions tend to work harder, train more, and push to exceed performance goals. Employees who are promoted are highly motivated, happy employees. A promotion is recognition of their work, usually includes a raise, and offers more prestige and corporate power. The corollary to this is also true. Employees that are passed by for a promotion are not happy and can become demotivated. Demotivation of employees that have been passed by for a promotion is an unavoidable risk. Since the business is a hierarchy and there are fewer available positions as employees move up in the hierarchy, it is not possible to promote everyone. This risk is mitigated by ensuring that the promotion policy of the business is as fair as possible and offers equal opportunity to all employees.

Current employees are a known entity compared to hiring from the outside. Promoting employees from within is a means of mitigating the risk of hiring the wrong employee. Current employees have already been trained and are familiar with the business's policies and procedures. The negative here is the loss of an opportunity to bring in new ideas from the outside that would come with hiring a new employee. *Does the business have a published promotion policy?*

Voluntary Terminations

Employees decide to leave their jobs for many reasons, such as career advancement, family or other personal situations, retirement, and job dissatisfaction. If an employee resigns, the business needs to request a signed resignation letter if the employee didn't provide one. This letter documents the termination as voluntary on the part of the employee, and it can be a source of data for reviewing the employment practices of the business. You might find it beneficial to read through some of the recent resignation letters as part of your due diligence. *Are resignation letters required from employees who voluntarily terminate their employment?*

Most businesses conduct exit interviews with terminating employees, but the results of these interviews are seldom reviewed by a management team. Furthermore, few exit interviews or termination letters get to see the light of day in any other manner. A management team needs to review all exit interviews to identify trends that will help mitigate the risk of further resignations. This feedback is critical when looking at the personnel infrastructure as a continuous process. *Is there a management team review of exit interview comments?*

Terminations for Cause

Acknowledging that particular employees aren't meeting the standards of employment and aren't responding to remediation and then taking the action to terminate those employees are difficult events for the employees, for their managers, and for the business. Terminations are often emotional events, and they present legal, financial, security, and even safety risks. The process that is followed for terminating employees for cause must be well thought out and documented, and managers who are involved with this process need to be trained. *Is there an established process for conducting a termination for cause, and are managers trained in executing this process?*

A termination for cause is generally performed only after it is determined that an employee is unable or unwilling to meet the standards of the business and a true attempt has been made to resolve the problem. It means that the business still has a need for the employee's job function and will have to hire someone else to fill the position. Hiring a new employee is costly and takes time so a termination for cause is always disruptive to the organization.

The process of terminating an employee for cause starts before the employee is even hired, at the point where the job requirements for the position are defined. Assuming that there were no unforeseeable personal changes with the employee that the hiring manager for this position failed to see, it means that the hiring manager failed to recognize the inability of the candidate to perform the job. This could reflect a problem with the hiring process, or it could reflect a skills problem with the manager. A termination for cause reflects on the manager as well as the employee, and feedback from the termination action needs to be tied back to the hiring process. The manager, for instance, might have assessed the employee's skills incorrectly, or failed to recognize that the employee lacked the experience to work with the team. What could have been done to prevent this situation from occurring? Hiring process changes or management training are potential risk mitigation actions. *Are hiring managers accountable when there is a termination for cause?*

When a manager determines that an employee has failed to meet his or her job standards, there needs to be an immediate consultation between the manager and HR to review the situation. This consultation is used to develop a plan to attempt to get the employee back on track with the manager's expectations. A termination for cause is generally the result of several discussions and notices advising the employee of the problem and telling the employee exactly what needs to be done to get back on track. A termination should never come as a surprise to an employee. This entire process, and specifically all employee performance notices, must be documented, and records of the written notices and the discussions with the employee need to be put in the employee's personnel folder. *Are employee performance notices given to the employees in writing and placed in their personnel folder?*

Performance discussions with employees are always difficult, and the further into the termination process, the greater the level of formality that needs to be employed. When holding a potentially contentious discussion with an employee, I advise managers to start the discussion by stating, "This will not be a good discussion." This notifies the employee up front about the nature of the discussion and removes the shock factor that these discussions can have. It sets the correct tone for the discussion from the beginning and lets the employee know this will be more than a chat. *Is there a list of all employees who are currently on performance notices?*

Terminations without Cause

Terminating employees without cause (layoffs) is a result of business fluctuations due to business performance cutbacks or retractions, staff changes due to project phase transitions, the loss of contracts, or the result of any other circumstance in which the business no longer needs the services of the employees even though the employees have otherwise met their job standards. Note that even when employees understand that layoffs may be coming, they may not expect the cutbacks to include them. Labor cutbacks resulting from terminations without cause reflect negatively on the market's perception of the business and create a brand risk for the business. "That business isn't growing. It just had an employee layoff." *Has the business had any labor reductions or terminations without cause? If so, when were they, and how many employees were involved?*

This type of termination is often softened by offering severance packages, job referrals, outplacement services, résumé writing services, and other packages aimed at helping the employees transition to new positions. These services help the terminated employees and also demonstrate the benevolence of the business to the remaining employees, helping to maintain their morale during what might otherwise be a stressful period. "Yes, we had to let people go, but see how well we took care of them." A common practice in these situations includes the use of a termination agreement that offers the termination benefits in return for the employees agreeing not to take any action against the business as a result of the termination. *What outstanding termination agreements does the business have?*

When a business offers termination packages, it may be establishing precedence for future terminations. The remaining employees expect that, in the event that they are also terminated, they will be given similar termination packages. With changes in management, changes in the economy, and changes in the financial position of the business, this may not be the case.

Where these expectations have been established, there is a risk if similar termination packages cannot be offered in the future. *Has there been any precedent or expectation established by the business for termination benefit packages?*

My comments are not intended to discourage businesses from offering termination packages to employees. Rather, it is important that the business consider its actions and clearly establish that the benefits it is providing at this time are not a precedent. The business does what it can at the time. It's also important, when possible, that the business explain to the remaining employees why these terminations occurred and that it address any questions about future job security issues. *Following a termination without cause, does the business explain the situation to the remaining employees?*

Occasionally an agreement is made between a business and key employees for them to remain on the job until some specified date or event, at which time the business promises to give the employees a retention bonus. "If you stay with us until after the acquisition, we will pay you a $50,000 bonus." Employment contracts formalize this type of arrangement, but often, where there is no employment contract, this type of offer is made verbally. The nature of any termination promises must be understood because they can have a future cost impact. *Have there been any formal or informal termination agreements made with existing employees?*

EMPLOYEE VALUE AND QUALITY

"Our employees are our most important asset." This statement makes for great press, particularly if you are one of the "most important assets." It's also one of the stock answers that assessment teams are likely to hear. It's a catch phrase that can also mean, "We're actually selling you our résumés." This is one of those bell-ringer phrases that may indicate that the BS Quotient is running a little high. A good employee team is of course one of the most important assets for any business, and it can take a long time to develop, but sustainable businesses also require infrastructure, intellectual property, products, and (of course) revenue along with the résumés. *Is there a résumé or CV on file for all employees?*

If your primary reason for investing in the business is to acquire its personnel assets, then hearing that the employees are the most important asset is a great message. If, however, you have other strategic reasons for the investment, such as acquiring a product line or customer base, then you need to be aware of what this statement could mean. If you're looking for a business with a mature operations infrastructure and expect that your investment will be more than résumé deep, then this statement is a risk indicator. The problem will be determining what the strengths of the employee team really are and what that means to the overall value you place on the business. Also, remember that résumés alone don't indicate the contributions the employees make to the business. *Is the value of the business limited to the strength of the employees' résumés?*

Product quality is a measure of how well the product complies with its defined requirements. Similarly, *employee quality* refers to the qualifications of the employees that enable them to perform the jobs to which they have been assigned. Having "a PhD on staff" can be an asset for a business. Having a PhD on staff who performs entry-level work usually isn't an effective personnel solution, and the PhD could be more of a liability than an asset. Obviously, this is a subjective description. Employee quality isn't just a question of college degrees. It's also a matter of the employees' past experience, both in the industry and in these positions, and it includes the compensation being paid for the work being performed. *Employee quality* refers to the overall value the employees bring to the business. *Does the business have the right people doing the right jobs?*

Over time, businesses tend to become top-heavy, having an imbalance between senior staff and entry-level employees. There needs to be a mixture of experienced, "high-end" employees supported by more junior, affordable employees, with the senior staff members holding leadership or management positions. *Does the business have a reasonable blend of labor grades?*

JOB PLACEMENT

In some businesses, everyone does a little bit of everything. In these situations, there's a tendency for the "dirty" jobs (the ones nobody wants to do) to get pushed off and not get done because they weren't specifically assigned to someone, or worse, senior employees waste time by getting bogged down doing the jobs that could have been assigned to their support staff. Getting the right people to do the right jobs starts with a definition of the jobs' requirements. It's important to discover whether the business has defined and staffed each position properly. *Are some people doing jobs that could be accomplished by other people in lower pay grades?*

I worked with a business that didn't use (or budget) administrative support. As a result there were many administrative tasks that just didn't get done efficiently, including such things as ordering team lunches, booking travel, and ordering office supplies. Management decided that the best way to get these tasks done was for the managers to divide up the tasks and do them themselves rather than leaving them to their staff members to do. When you add up the time and the salaries of the managers to do these tasks each week, they probably could have afforded to hire two administrators for the same amount. Nevertheless, the near-term benefit of this was tremendous. The employees recognized that the managers were willing to take on any tasks that needed to be done. I don't recommend this approach as a long-term solution, but for the short term, it showed great management involvement. *Is management engaged to help solve staff problems?*

As another example of how things sometimes are worked out: I had been asked to help a small technology business that was facing some real product quality challenges. It took almost a year to turn this business around. One day the receptionist came into my office almost in tears and ready to resign. She said it was bad enough that she had to put up with calls from irate customers, but she was no longer going to tolerate one of my manager's constantly complaining about the way she handled customer calls. She said, "He just doesn't understand how difficult my job is." I sat at her desk for an hour answering the phone. It was the toughest hour I spent with that business. I asked all of my managers to take a turn doing her job. None lasted very long at it, and the offending manager never complained again. I recognized the role she was playing in improving our customer satisfaction, and I gave her an immediate raise. It's an absolute necessity for managers to understand the nature and extent of the job they are asking employees to perform. *Do managers understand the full extent of the jobs their staff members perform?*

A written job description identifies the responsibilities and duties of each employee, and it shows that management has at least taken the time to plan what needs to be done and what skills will be required. Job descriptions allow managers to place the correct people in the jobs and give other employees the opportunity to see the requirements for their next promotion.

When conducting your assessment, remember that job descriptions can take on many forms. Job descriptions can be captured in the classified ads placed for hiring new employees, or they can be written statements posted in the break room. Employment contracts that include job descriptions may also exist for key personnel. Whatever the method used for documenting job descriptions, they need to be applied consistently across the business with some level of formality. Some large businesses keep a skills database to help locate employees with latent skills to be called upon when needed for short-term assignments rather than hiring additional staff. Discovering that the business keeps a skills database is an indicator of process maturity and an indicator that the business has given some thought to the long-term staffing plans needed to manage their growth. *Does the business maintain a skills database?*

THE HERO EMPLOYEE

Some employees always go above and beyond their defined requirements and put in a heroic effort, no matter what job they're given. These employees become the hero employees of any business. When they're called on, they are the employees who never turn down a task and never say no. If you ask, they will be there. You often hear they have taken on a job because "it just needed to get done." As managers, we would like to have all of our employees be this type of superstar. So what could be wrong with this kind of dedication? Nothing, if it is in response to a specific call for help. Unfortunately, not all employees are heroes, which often means that managers are overrelying on those employees who are.

Problems can arise if the hero employees become the channels through which all activities have to pass. This can create choke points and a dependence that can hurt team performance, and it can also put the business at tremendous risk should the hero employees decide to leave. It can create problems with otherwise good employees as well who become frustrated and annoyed if they start to see the heroes as threats (by their actions, the heroes change what had been acceptable standards for the job). In these situations, the hero employees can create a performance risk for the overall employee team. Furthermore, why should the other employees put in any extra effort if the hero employees are going to get all the accolades and opportunities! As for the hero employees, they often end up with so many tasks to do that it causes work to become unbalanced across the team. *Are there any identified employee workflow bottlenecks?*

The loss of hero employees is always a risk, and the business needs to take extra steps to mitigate this risk. For critical staff positions, the business needs to consider *key employee insurance* (with the business as the beneficiary) for any individual that the company depends on, and it may be a good idea to put these people under employment contracts. *What has been done to protect the business against the loss of key employees?*

EMPLOYEE MOTIVATION

Employee motivation and management effectiveness have been the subjects of many books. A search of the Internet for motivational speakers will return thousands of listings. I am occasionally asked to conduct these types of sessions. Many things, including money, recognition, prestige, and numerous other forms of family and personal rewards are used to motivate employees. Surprisingly, money isn't always at the top of the list. It's also rarely at the bottom! These incentives are intended to reward employees for going above and beyond the minimum requirements of their job. *What incentive programs are in place to motivate employees to go above and beyond to help the business succeed?*

Employees are hired for their skills, and they are expected to diligently perform their jobs. In return, employees expect to be paid fairly for their work. Motivated employees have the desire to excel at their jobs. Their desire for both personal success and for the success of the business brings an added level of passion to their work. Simply put, motivated employees set personal goals beyond those required by the job and take personal initiative to achieve their goals. They tie their personal success to the success of the business. Unfortunately, we also find situations in which there is peer pressure to just meet the standard for the job but not go beyond. This is common in organized labor situations. "If you exceed the standard, they'll expect everyone to exceed it." *Do the employees tie their personal success to the success of the business?*

Employee performance is similar to that of athletes. There are lots of good athletes and plenty of good employees, but there are two things that are required to make great athletes or great employees. Great athletes possess both skill and desire. Similarly, employees who have the skills to do their job and the desire to see the company succeed are more productive than those with the same skills but without the desire for success. Business is a team sport. Employees need to desire success for the business as well as for themselves. Employees need to have a passion for the success of the business. As many coaches would tell you, when there is a choice between skill and desire, they would much rather have people with the desire to win. They can teach them the skills. Motivation is used to create and reinforce the employees' desire for the business to succeed. *Do employees display a passion to go above and beyond for the success of the business?*

Motivated managers also bring passion to the job and are best able to motivate their teams. The goals of management and the goals of the business need to be closely aligned. Occasionally, the actions and comments of individual managers don't reflect the interests of the business. There is a risk in these situations that the employees will become more loyal to their managers than to the business. This can be a risk if the managers' personal goals are contrary to those of the business or if there is an anticipated management change due to an M&A event. *Are the goals of the management team aligned with those of the business?*

Management goals need to be established on a periodic basis (for example, yearly or quarterly), and they should be agreed to by the business and the managers. When goal setting is handled as a negotiation between the managers and the business, the resulting goals are realistic, clearly understood, measured, and within the managers' control to accomplish. *Does the business have a management goal setting policy?*

EMPLOYEE STABILITY

Employee stability refers to the ability of the business to retain employees, particularly key employees, who possess critical skills needed for the continued operation and success of the business. High employee turnover can have a significant morale and performance impact as well as a high budget impact. This expense includes the direct costs of finding and training new staff members and the indirect costs of things like the lost intellectual property that walks out the door along with the employees. In highly competitive markets, employee "job hopping" can present a serious risk because it can artificially inflate the cost of labor. Employee retention plans can take on many forms including compensation analysis and employment contracts. Additional methods for improving employee retention include putting employment contracts in place with key staff members, stock options tied to continued employment, and ensuring that an environment exists that entices the employees to stay (including proper motivation and compensation). *Does the business have an employee retention plan? Are there employment contracts for all key employees?*

One of my former clients was a business that had coffee mugs made that said "No Whining" in large red letters across the cup. During an all-hands meeting, the business handed the cups out to the entire staff. Everyone thought the mugs were funny, but the mugs were intended to solve a growing employee problem. The true and sad fact was that management had been unable to keep a few, very vocal, disenfranchised employees from degrading the morale of the rest of the staff. The constant complaining by these vocal employees resulted in a high staff turnover rate, resulting in tremendous risk for the project. Of course, the critical employees with the most salable skills were the first to leave, which then resulted in an increasingly late schedule and increased stress on a major project. Nothing that had been done for these employees seemed to be sufficient to silence their complaints, including introducing 9/80 work schedules, out-of-cycle raises, task completion bonuses, and even membership in a local health club. The whining had become cultural.

The critical employees knew they had the business on the defensive, and they were taking every advantage they could get. Of course, in hindsight, the employees who left the business first were the highly skilled critical employees who had no trouble finding other jobs. The lesser skilled critical employees who remained with the project continued complaining, only louder as the stress continued to grow. They were the ones who were probably having trouble finding other employment for various reasons or they would also have resigned. Had the business realized the negative impact that a few employees were able to have, it could have acted sooner and let this group go early enough for the project to recover. The problem was finally resolved by sending the project to a different division at another location, cutting the entire staff, and completely shutting down the original facility. Can you imagine what the cost of this was and the impact on the reputation of the business! It was clearly a tug-of-war with the employees taking no ownership for the success of the project or the business.

A staffing curve that shows numbers of employees over time can also be revealing. Many fluctuations in the staffing curve result from normal business events, such as the completion of a major project. Employee cutbacks are also seasonal and normal for some businesses. Occasionally, however, setbacks occur because of unplanned events, poor sales performance, or market downturns that result in cutbacks that were not planned by the business. These types of changes to the staffing curve can reveal periods during which the business hasn't performed well, and they are indicators that more exploration should be done. *Does the staffing curve correlate with downturns in the profitability of the business?*

EMPLOYEE TRAINING

Employee training programs ensure that employees are working efficiently and in compliance with established government, industry, and business standards. Unfortunately, training is often conducted in an ad hoc manner and given only as an afterthought or out of sheer necessity. Training needs to be conducted according to a training plan, and the cost of executing the plan needs to be budgeted. *What employee training is required, and does the business have an annual training plan?*

In some industries, periodic professional training certifications are required. If this is the case, the business needs to maintain a training schedule and track the required training in order to avoid potential fines or other liabilities from loss of certification. *What professional certifications do employees require, and is there a schedule for tracking required recertifications?*

If the employee training expense wasn't included in the operations budget, then the training will likely not be performed. Training expenses are generally tracked as an overhead expense, and the result is that training has a double impact on the business. If the business is selling labor hours (direct charges to a contract), such as on a government contract, it will lose the billable revenue that could have been charged while the employees are in class. At the same time, the business will be paying the overhead hourly rate for the employee (an indirect overhead expense) during the training.

Training expenses include the cost of the instructor, course preparation and materials, and the labor cost for employees attending a class. Training is expensive, but it is absolutely required as risk mitigation that helps improve the sustainability of the business. *Are employee training expenses included as budget items for all groups?*

Formalized training classes are justifiable because they shorten the training curve resulting from on-the-job training (OJT). OJT can be a risk because it seems less expensive and is therefore often conducted without management identifying clear training requirements and goals. In these cases, the true cost of OJT can be buried in inefficiency, poor quality, and operational risks that are not easily measured. OJT risks can be mitigated by identifying the requirements (known as *key learning objectives*) of the OJT program. Employee training is a key to building efficient infrastructures and mitigating risk. *Does the business identify key learning objectives when it offers on-the-job training programs?*

Because there is a double cost impact for training, many businesses try to find ways to be creative in scheduling their training sessions. Creative training approaches include the use of brown bag lunches for which training sessions are conducted during company-provided luncheons, evening and weekend classes, and online training that the employees complete from home. This usually raises an issue. Is the business correct in asking the employees to complete training on their own time? These solutions may have legal or ethical implications depending on the labor classification of the employees, and the business should have reviewed the legality of its training solutions.

I have generally felt that off-hours training is not a problem if the training can reasonably be considered professional development and it provides career benefits to the employees as well as to the business. The purpose for the training should be considered to determine whether it is unique to the business or could reasonably be considered career development. Training needed for professional licenses or certifications, particularly if the employees are likely to mention their licenses or certifications on their next résumé, seems justifiable as off-hours training. Completing this type of training, on the employees' own time, could easily be considered an employment requirement. The business is paying for the training, and it could have expected the employees to complete this training as a prerequisite of their employment. Asking the employees to take a training course in the use of a proprietary database that is not likely to be used anywhere else needs to be done on business time. If the business requires off-hours training, it should be identified as part of the hiring process—that is,

as a term of employment—so that the employees understand the requirements for putting in their own time to complete the training. *What creative
employee training methods does the business use?*

Employee mentoring programs are also used as another creative way
to control training expenses. A mentoring program teams less experienced
employees with more experienced mentor employees. Generally this type
of training program is conducted one-on-one between the mentors and stu-
dents. All of the previous comments regarding the risks and mitigation of
OJT programs also apply here. Mentoring programs are often used in situations in which a poor trainee decision could result in a serious safety risk
or a risk of harm to the business operations. In these situations, mentors
are able to closely monitor the actions of the trainees. *Is there a formalized
mentoring program in place for employee training and advancement?*

The need for training isn't limited to the development of employee
skills. More and more, employee training is also used as a type of insurance, in areas such as ethics and HR practices, where the business has
some level of liability due to employee actions. In these cases, training is
conducted as a form of risk mitigation. By providing ethics training, the
business demonstrates that its ethics policy clearly forbids certain types of
behaviors, potentially limiting the business's liability if an employee vio-
lates an ethics rule. The business can establish that the training is evidence
that it doesn't condone the employee's behavior and that it attempted to
protect against such actions. This may be a reasonable way to mitigate the
risk from this type of litigation if the business also establishes a record for
enforcing compliance of the policy.

In order to properly match the job skills of employees to the knowledge required to efficiently perform their job, the training plan needs to
identify the curricula necessary for the employees. *Does employee training include the business policies for each infrastructure area?*

When training is scheduled, attendees should be expected to be in the classroom on time and to stay throughout each entire training session.

Training is expensive. The justification for this expense is the
improvement in employee efficiency and the potential risk mitigation it

provides for the business. And yet, in spite of these advantages, I have attended (and conducted) many training courses that were treated like optional social events for the attendees. Managers seem to be the worst offenders in this, and they often miss the opportunity to show tremendous leadership. Sustainable businesses establish standards for their training sessions. When training is scheduled, attendees should be expected to be in the classroom on time and to stay throughout each entire training session. Cell phones and laptop computers should be turned off unless they are used as part of the class. *Does the business measure its training effectiveness?*

Summary of the Personnel Infrastructure Questions

1. What is the longevity and average turnover rate of employees?
2. What government regulations affect the employee benefit packages today and in the foreseeable future?
3. How does the business proactively monitor changing regulations that could impact its legal, financial, and operations infrastructure?
4. Does the business publish a list of employee benefits?
5. Are there any anticipated changes in the employee benefit plan?
6. What fringe benefits does the business offer its employees?
7. Does the business conduct an annual benefits review and planning session?
8. Is the annual growth in employee compensation planned, and has it been budgeted?
9. What compensation packages do employees currently receive including both salary and benefits?
10. Are employee salaries subject to collective bargaining?
11. How does the business track all of the elements of its employees' compensation?
12. Does the business analyze the competitive salary range for each position or conduct a periodic review of the cost of benefits to ensure that its compensation rates are competitive?
13. How does the business establish the salary and benefit guidelines for the next year?
14. Have all promised compensation increases been documented and included in the compensation plan?

15. What is the working relationship between the employees and the business?
16. Are there any existing agreements with organized labor?
17. Are there any known or ongoing actions to organize employees within the business?
18. Does the business review its employment practices on an annual basis?
19. Are there established processes for hiring and terminating employees?
20. Are personnel actions and discussions documented in the employee personnel files?
21. Does the business follow a documented staffing policy?
22. Are there any outstanding employee sign-on incentives? If so, what is their value, and when do they mature?
23. Is training required for all employees who are involved in the recruiting process?
24. Are background searches conducted for all employment candidates?
25. Are all applicants required to fill out a standardized application form?
26. Is there a single point of control for all staffing decisions?
27. Does the business have a policy controlling employment offers?
28. Is there an established process for conducting employee performance appraisals?
29. Are performance appraisals tied to increases in salary and/or bonuses, and how has the business planned for these increases?
30. Are managers trained to conduct effective performance appraisals?
31. Does the business have performance appraisals for each employee for the preceding three years?
32. Does the business have a published promotion policy?
33. Are resignation letters required from employees who voluntarily terminate their employment?
34. Is there a management team review of exit interview comments?
35. Is there an established procedure for conducting a termination for cause, and are managers trained in executing this process?
36. Are hiring managers accountable when there is a termination for cause?

37. Are employee performance notices given in writing and placed in their personnel folder?
38. Is there a list of all employees who are currently on performance notices?
39. Has the business had any labor reductions or terminations without cause? If so, when were they, and how many employees were involved?
40. What outstanding termination agreements does the business have?
41. Has there been any precedent or expectation established for termination benefit packages?
42. Following a termination without cause, does the business explain the situation to the remaining employees?
43. Have there been any formal or informal termination agreements made with existing employees?
44. Is there a résumé or CV on file for all employees?
45. Is the value of the business limited to the strength of the employee's résumés?
46. Does the business have the right people doing the right jobs?
47. Does the business have a reasonable blend of labor grades?
48. Are some people doing jobs that could be accomplished by other people in lower pay grades?
49. Is management engaged to help solve staff problems?
50. Do managers understand the full extent of the jobs their staff members perform?
51. Does the business maintain a skills database?
52. Are there any identified employee workflow bottlenecks?
53. What has been done to protect the business against the loss of key employees?
54. What incentive programs are in place to motivate employees to go above and beyond to help the business succeed?
55. Do the employees tie their personal success to the success of the business?
56. Do employees display a passion to go above and beyond for the success of the business?
57. Are the goals of the management team aligned with those of the business?
58. Does the business have a management goal setting policy?

59. Does the business have an employee retention plan?
60. Are there employment contracts for all key employees?
61. Does the staffing curve correlate with downturns in the profitability of the business?
62. What employee training is required, and does the business have an annual training plan?
63. What professional certifications do employees require, and is there a schedule for tracking required recertifications?
64. Are employee training expenses included as budget items for all groups?
65. Does the business identify key learning objectives when it offers on-the-job training programs?
66. What creative employee training methods does the business use?
67. Is there a formalized mentoring program in place for employee training and advancement?
68. Does employee training include the business policies for each infrastructure area?
69. Does the business measure its training effectiveness?

CHAPTER 10

Assessment of the Financial Infrastructure

In 2001 we saw the collapse of the Enron Corporation and eventually the conviction of several of its senior managers for accounting fraud. Along with the collapse of Enron, and as a direct result of Enron's failure, we also saw the collapse of Arthur Andersen, which had been Enron's external audit firm. Arthur Andersen was one of the "big five" accounting firms, and its reputation was fatally tied to Enron. Arthur Andersen's defense was that it could work only with the numbers provided to it by Enron, that its reports were based on accepted accounting practices, and therefore, that its work was sound. Unfortunately, during the Enron investigation, Arthur Andersen destroyed documents related to the case, and the firm was eventually convicted of obstruction of justice.

The implication in Arthur Andersen's statement was that the financial infrastructure of Enron was at fault rather than Arthur Andersen's own accounting practices. Enron had incorrectly assessed the future value of some of its contracts, and it had mislabeled some of its existing assets to hide its losses. The operational procedures that could have provided Enron with checks and balances to control its financial infrastructure were flawed, arguably intentionally, and, as a result, the company produced flawed financial data for Arthur Andersen to work from. The Enron financial infrastructure didn't include a sufficient control structure to ensure that the financial operation of the business stayed within the bounds set by the Securities and Exchange Commission (SEC) for large public corporations. Regardless of the size of a business, whether it is a large public entity that must comply with the SEC rules or a small privately owned business that must properly file its taxes, there must be a financial infrastructure in place that establishes a framework that will guide and control its financial operations.

Within *Operations Due Diligence* I make a distinction between financial due diligence and Operations Due Diligence of the financial infrastructure. Financial due diligence is an assessment, performed by auditors and accountants, to establish a current, correct valuation of the business. Financial due diligence assesses the fiscal status of the business at a point in time.

Operations due diligence of the financial infrastructure, in contrast, is an assessment of the continuing financial operations of the business. It is the assessment that was never done for Enron! It is an assessment of the financial control structures that form the framework of the business's financial operations.

Financial due diligence assumes that the operations of the business will remain constant while the performance of the business will change in response to external influences such as changes in the market. During financial due diligence, for example, an income statement might project an increase in sales revenue; but by itself, it doesn't tell investors whether the increase was due to a change in the marketing strategy of the business (causing greater market penetration) or growth of the market (due to an unrelated increase in the number of customers). Further analysis is required to determine what caused this change in the financial performance of the business. Did revenue go up because the market expanded or because operational changes resulted in increased market penetration? This type of analysis is accomplished only through Operations Due Diligence, which assesses the events that caused the change and, as a result, will identify potential risks or opportunities resulting from these events.

> Nothing in this book is intended to replace the need for a full financial due diligence assessment from a certified financial auditor.

The financial infrastructure defines the system used for managing finances as part of the day-to-day operation of the business. There is a clear linkage between financial due diligence and due diligence of the financial infrastructure. The Enron collapse clearly demonstrated that. As Arthur Andersen found out, though, looking at the numbers alone is not sufficient. There must also be an operational assessment of the financial infrastructure that looks at how the numbers were arrived at.

The financial assessment relies on the validity of the financial data that supports the valuation. The operations assessment looks at the underlying mechanisms that are used to generate the data on a continuous basis. If the financial infrastructure of the business is flawed, then the financial data created by it will also likely be flawed and therefore so will the results of the financial assessment. Conversely, an operations assessment is not concerned with how the data is used; it is concerned with how the data is created. It assesses the procedures that are used to create the data, and from this, it looks for indications in the data that might provide clues about the future operations of the business.

FINANCIAL AUTHORITY AND RESPONSIBILITY

Financial authority needs to be clearly defined and controlled. The authority and limitation of each manager to make financial commitments need to be published as a policy by the senior financial officer, and individual managers need to be given written notification, informing them about the limits of their financial signature authority and authorizing them to spend within these limits. *Does each manager have a defined and documented level of financial signature authority?*

All businesses need to identify an individual as its senior financial officer. This may be a chief financial officer (CFO), or it may be another officer, such as the president, who holds this responsibility. *Who is the senior financial officer of the business?*

The senior financial officer is delegated the ultimate responsibility for financial control and has the authority to determine the fiscal direction of the business. Financial authority is then delegated from this person across the organization. The size and legal structure of the business also affect the ability of the business to delegate its financial authority. *Is there a written policy that defines the rules for financial commitment of the business?*

Starting in 2002, the delegation of financial authority was given a new sense of urgency for public corporations, requiring them to comply with the Sarbanes-Oxley Act (known as SOX). SOX was enacted in response to the Enron collapse, and it mandates that senior executives take individual responsibility for the accuracy and completeness of corporate financial reports. It was intended to protect shareholders of public corporations from fraudulent accounting practices and to create transparency into the business.

SOX establishes rules for the financial operations of public corporations. SOX also has a potential impact on privately owned businesses if they intend to go public at some point in the future. There is a tremendous cost and time impact of SOX, and if your plan is to take the business public at some point, you must be aware of the impact SOX could have on the business. To become a public entity, the business will have to implement a financial infrastructure capable of complying with the requirements of SOX. This can be a significant risk for small corporations and businesses, keeping some businesses from remaining as public entities while keeping others from ever becoming public entities. *Does the business need to comply with the Sarbanes-Oxley Act, or does it anticipate a future compliance requirement?*

Sarbanes-Oxley will have a cost impact on privately owned businesses if they plan on going public in the future, and investors must be aware of this impact.

SOX is administered by the Securities and Exchange Commission, which publishes the rules for compliance. SOX impacts the operations of the information management (IM) infrastructure along with the financial infrastructure because it defines the financial records that the business must archive. SOX mandates that all business records, including electronic records and electronic messages, must be saved for "not less than five years." The consequences for noncompliance are fines and imprisonment, or both. IT departments are increasingly faced with the challenge of creating and maintaining a corporate records archive capable of meeting these requirements. Remember, even if the business is not a public corporation but anticipates becoming public at some point, its financial infrastructure must be able to support the SOX regulations.

SOX mandates three rules that affect the operations of the business and the management of its electronic records. The first rule deals with the destruction, alteration, or falsification of records. *How does the business enforce the collection and archiving of Sarbanes-Oxley compliant data?*

The second rule defines the retention period for records storage as five years. Best practices indicate that corporations securely store all business records using the same guidelines set for public accountants including "all audit or review work papers for a period of five years from the end of the fiscal period in which the audit or review was concluded." *What is the cost for retention and archiving of Sarbanes-Oxley compliant data and reports?*

The third rule refers to the type of information that needs to be stored and covers all business records and communications "including electronic communications, records such as work papers, documents that form the basis of an audit or review, memoranda, correspondence, communications, other documents, and records (including electronic records) which are created, sent, or received in connection with an audit or review and contain conclusions, opinions, analyses, or financial data relating to such an audit or review." *How does the business audit its Sarbanes-Oxley compliance?*

OPERATIONS LINKAGES TO THE P&L, BALANCE SHEET, AND CASH FLOW REPORTS

The profit and loss (P&L), balance sheet, and cash flow reports are the key documents used to conduct the financial assessment and valuation of a business. These reports are generally thought of as the domain of accounting and are core to the financial due diligence, but they also play an important role in operations and the Operations Due Diligence. The goal of your assessment will be to validate the sources of the data contained in these documents and explore the implications of this data on the future operations of the business. For instance, what is the process for making sales projections or the policy for qualifying travel expenses? While there are separate goals for the financial and operations assessments, they need to be conducted in the context of one another. *Has the accuracy of the business's financial reports been validated?*

Not surprisingly, when speaking with investors, businesses tend to understate their expenses and overstate their revenues. Also, not surprisingly, they tend to do the opposite on their taxes! For this reason, prior tax returns are an important verification of the business's financial claims. *Do the prior tax returns support the business's income and expense claims?*

Financial reports are not prepared solely for the due diligence assessment or for the use of the financial group within the business. The P&L, balance sheet, and cash flow reports also need to be used by managers as tools that support their day-to-day operations decisions and to help managers identify trends within their group. All managers should be familiar with these tools to enable them to monitor and plan their group's performance. An excellent reference for managers trying to understand the operational use of the financial tools in detail is John A. Tracy's *How to Read a Financial Report: For Managers, Entrepreneurs, Lenders, Lawyers, and Investors*, seventh edition (Wiley, 2009).

P&L Reports

P&L reports capture the actual sales revenues and the actual incurred expenses of the business for a given period of time. Most businesses create a P&L report at each management level within the organization (depending on the structure of the business). The reports are then rolled up into a summary for the entire business. The P&L report summarizes the performance of each group, generally on a month-by-month basis. They are based on the actual expenses and earnings at each organizational level. Managers can use these reports to validate their expenditures against their budgets and ensure the proper allocation of expenses to cost accounts. *Do all group managers review their P&L reports on a periodic basis?*

P&L reports are used as guides to help managers make near-term expenditure decisions. If the P&L reports are tracked over time, they provide a means for analyzing revenue, expense, and earnings trends of the organization. For example, "Am I overspending my travel budget to generate the current revenue?" By looking at the P&L trends, this type of financial performance data can be used to make tactical operational decisions to help mitigate near-term risk and capture opportunities for the business. *Do the revenue, expense, or earnings trends reflected in the P&L reports indicate any operational risks or opportunities?*

Balance Sheets

The balance sheet summarizes the assets and liabilities of the business at a specified point in time. Assets include the means of production, such as the equipment and facilities used, and liabilities include payables, such as the amounts owed to suppliers. The balance sheet can be used as an indicator that the business is either under- or overcapitalized, supporting strategic decisions about the allocation of resources needed to support future plans. For instance, did the business sell critical automation equipment recently to boost its cash reserves as part of its positioning for investors (a short-term tactical decision but not a good strategic decision)? *Does the balance sheet identify any operational risks or opportunities for the business?*

Again, for the operations assessment, you are looking at these reports for operational discovery rather than for the financial valuation of the business. A balance sheet needs to be created just prior to closing on the investment because you need a current statement of the business's assets and liabilities. Does the balance sheet indicate any operational risks or opportunities such as not having the capital to purchase needed manufacturing equipment or components? If so, will this still be true after the investment? Comparing the balance sheets over several years provides historic trends, which can be valuable assessment tools. *Have the cash reserves dwindled over time?*

Cash Flow Statements

The cash flow statement shows the cash reserves available to support the operations of the business. This report reveals a lot about the day-to-day fiscal management of the business. If it includes historic data (at least the prior year's operations), it is an indicator of how well the business has planned and managed its cash. The cash flow statement is used by management as a tactical rather than strategic tool. It shows the rise and fall of available cash needed to meet the near-term operational requirements, and it can be used to support an analysis of both the business's accounts receivable (AR) and its accounts payable (AP). *Has the business established a track record for timely collection of its accounts receivable? Has the business established a track record for meeting its accounts payable obligations on time?*

Because labor costs are the largest expense of many businesses, it is important to assess the business's ability to generate sufficient cash flow to support its payroll expenses. Failure to meet payroll is an obvious risk (or opportunity, depending on your investment goals). *Has the business failed to make any of its past payroll expenses in a timely manner?*

The cash flow statement isn't a measure of business performance. Managers often confuse the cash flow statement as a statement of the profits rather than as an operations indicator. For instance, products financed by the business on credit terms rather than for cash or a payroll that is drawn from a bank line of credit will reflect the performance of the business on the balance sheet, but it would be misleading when looked at strictly through the cash flow statement.

Managers can use the cash flow statements to determine how to meet their operational cash needs at the time they need them. *Are cash flow statements regularly used to predict operational cash needs?*

Managing Cash Reserves

Every business faces the challenge of managing its cash reserves. A business can support its needs for cash by depleting its cash reserves, by drawing against a line of credit, by seeking funds from outside investors, or by selling its products. Ideally, all operations will be supported by sales revenues. The problem with this, however, is that sales revenues lag operational expenses, and there is a risk that needed resources will not be available at the time they are needed. *Are revenue projections available for at least the next three years?*

The cost to develop a product occurs well before the product is sold, leaving the expense for current operations to be justified against future sales revenues. Estimating future sales revenue accurately therefore is important because the projections are used to justify the current cash expenditures and investments of the business. Businesses create pro forma projections based on their prior sales history of similar products. A *pro forma projection* is an estimate of the value of future sales. Some businesses provide projections without creating a detailed specification of the exact terms of the sales. If the projection, for example, is for "$50,000 in sales revenue," does that mean 50 units at $1,000 or 1,000 units at $50? This type of imprecision could present an obvious operational risk if the details of the projections are not understood and the projections are broad generalizations. *How much detail is behind the business's pro forma projections?*

The business may be in a position where sales will increase while revenue does not. There could, for instance, be sales based on a customer's line of credit with terms allowing the customer to make payments over time.

This could create an increase in production costs while there is a lag in the actual cash receipts. If the business is planning a sudden ramp-up in production, it could result in unidentified or unsupported operations resource needs. There must be a bridge between the cash receipts and the operational resources needed to support expenses (such as production and marketing, which must be expensed much earlier in time). *Does the business track the time-to-market for each product line?*

If the business projects a linear revenue growth, such as 20 to 30 percent per year over the next three years, this likely represents a sustainable low-risk growth, with reasonable expansion of operations supported by sales. If, however, there is a point where the curve indicates a radical increase in the projected revenues (referred to as a *hockey stick* because of the shape of the revenue curve), then a strong rationale should be provided to justify why this growth will suddenly occur (see Figure 10.1). More important, there must be an equivalent plan for ramping up the operations infrastructure to support the expanded operations requirements. *If the projections show hockey stick growth, is there a rationale to support this increase, and is there an equivalent ramp-up in the operations expenses of the business?*

There is a performance risk if revenue projections are driven from the top down. Revenue projections need to be developed by the sales team and tied directly to management's performance goals and sales quotas. When these figures come from the sales team, the sales team takes ownership of the projections and is pressured to make them realistic. The projections can then be rolled up across all of the sales territories to provide a valid overall estimate. On a frequent basis, the sales pipeline needs to be examined to determine whether or not it can support the revenue

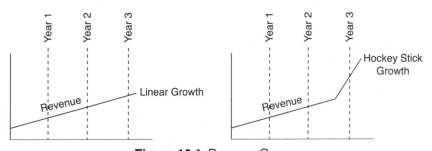

Figure 10.1 Revenue Curves

projections. If it cannot, it indicates that further assessment into areas, such as lead flow trends, may need to be performed. *Is the marketing lead flow sufficient to support the revenue projections?*

Pro forma means "according to form."
Sales pro forma means "according to the projected sales." Sales that are not projected, such as an unanticipated opportunity, are outside the pro forma figures.

The term *pro forma* might be another risk indicator or an indicator that the BS Quotient is in play. *Pro forma revenue projections* are forecasts of future sales revenues. These projections are based on anticipated sales activities, and they would not include revenues from *bluebirds*—that is, revenues that are not anticipated but rather "drop in." Businesses are tempted to report all revenues from the previous year (their actual revenues) to potential investors without explaining that the expenses associated with those revenues were also one-time, nonrecurring expenses. They include *bluebird revenues*. They were not in last year's pro forma projections, but the revenue from the bluebirds is included in this year's sales variance figures. This indicates a potential risk if last year's actual expenses reflect the effort to generate non–pro forma sales. If a business tells you that these are profits from pro forma sales, it may also be stating that it had not accounted for some expenses when calculating profit because the expenses were unanticipated, nonrecurring expenses, not tied directly to the pro forma sales. You need to question both sides of the equation! Depending on your investment goals, you may also want to ask for pro forma reports in order to determine the normal operations of the business. *Is the business reporting all sales and all operating expenses, or is it making pro forma adjustments?*

Budgets

Budgets are the primary tool for financial planning and control. A budget is an educated estimate of anticipated expenses needed to achieve the projected level of performance. All managers with financial responsibility need to be working from a budget that they helped create. *Are budgets created at each operational level of the organization?*

Unless this is a new business or a new product line with no historic expense data, budgets should be created from a baseline of prior operating expenses. "I know how much my telephone expenses were last year, so I have a basis on which to estimate these expenses in next year's budget." The finance group needs to prepare a draft budget for each manager from historic cost data. *Are budgets created using historic records of prior expenses?*

In some businesses the budget is created by the finance group and given to the managers to work from. This is often the case when managers have grown out of technical or manufacturing positions where they haven't previously had to deal with fiscal management. It's not uncommon to hear managers say, "I let the finance team handle the numbers." There is a risk when the finance department creates the budget because the managers may not take ownership of the budget. When the managers exceed the budget, they can say, "That wasn't my budget. It is what I was given." If the managers don't have ownership of their budget, they don't feel bound by it. It's much different if they have exceeded their own estimate. *Do functional managers own their budgets, or does finance create their budgets for them?*

Budgets are guidelines that help manage operational expenses. When managers have ownership of their budget, they can be held accountable for their performance against the budget. Managers also need to be given the freedom to execute according to their approved plan. Passing financial authority down the management chain is difficult in some organizations where the top level retains the complete financial authority and doesn't pass it down to the lower levels. This creates a performance risk because it's difficult to hold the midlevel managers accountable if they haven't been given control. This is an example of allocating responsibility without authority. When this situation is found, it is an indicator that the business has a weak financial infrastructure as well as potential trust and budgeting issues. *Is financial authority delegated to all managers to execute their operations plan according to their approved budget?*

In most businesses the budget process is an iterative process. It starts with revenue projections and an allocated profit goal at the highest level. Performance goals are created from these and allocated down the management chain to all levels to be used for the creation of each group's detailed budget. Budgets eventually become a negotiation with individual managers of the expenses they will incur in order to meet their goals. Exploring the method used for creating and allocating budgets will help you understand the financial control system of the business. *How are budget performance goals established?*

Budgets need to include a list of assumptions made by the managers during their creation. This is helpful in the event that there are false assumptions, unforeseen environmental changes, or other unplanned events that alter the budget baseline, causing deviations from the plan that were not envisioned. Eventually, individual managers will report their performance against the budget. If deviations are encountered that were not within the managers' control, then reviewing the original assumptions may indicate the source of an estimation problem. *Do managers document their budget assumptions?*

Some businesses treat budgets as fixed and unchanging. Unfortunately, not all business events can be foreseen, and budgets need to be able to support the changing needs of the business. This is particularly true in technology markets that change quickly. A budget is a baseline that should not be changed simply because there was a deviation from it. If there is a valid reason to make a change, however, then there must be a mechanism for revising the budget baseline. If the business is partway into the year, for instance, and it becomes clear that it needs to revise its strategic plan due to an unanticipated shift in the market, then the managers need to have a change control mechanism for modifying the budget, either reducing it to reflect the realities of a poor market or increasing it to support expanded development needs and opportunities if sales projections are being exceeded (yes, it happens!). "We recognized a sudden market shift toward products like ours and revised the budget to increase our marketing along with our increased projections."

If the budget is fixed and there is no change mechanism, then the budget becomes obsolete as soon as there is an event that changes the plan. The budget is a tool against which accurate business decisions need to be made, and its effectiveness diminishes if it isn't able to remain current with the plan. Budget changes should not be made simply to match poor performance. If a budget change request mechanism exists, it allows finance to balance budgets among departments if possible, and it also ensures that a review of the rationale for the changes will occur. *Is there a mechanism for modifying the budget in response to the changing operational needs of the business?*

Some businesses anticipate budget change requests and hold a *management reserve* to handle these changes. This is particularly true in highly turbulent markets as is frequently seen in the software industry where market response to competition can occur quickly or where evolutionary development methods are used. In these cases, the business knows that strategic changes will occur but not the extent of the changes. There is a risk because it's difficult to determine whether sufficient reserve has been held in these situations. A management reserve exists when the top-down budget allocation holds back some percentage of the anticipated expenses rather than fully allocating them down to the groups. For instance, to reach its profit goals, a business expects its expenses to be around $1 million. It allocates $800,000 down to the groups and reserves $200,000 in anticipation of some unforeseen events. *Does the business hold a management reserve?*

PROGRAM OR PROJECT MANAGEMENT

The use of the terms *program manager* and *project manager* is often industry dependent. Within *Operations Due Diligence*, they are interchangeable, and any tendency toward one or the other is purely coincidental.

Program or project managers (PM) provide the bridge between the finance group and the other functional groups. PMs differ from functional managers in that they perform an operations role (similar to that of general manager), focusing solely on the projects they are assigned. PMs are matrix managers, responsible for marshaling all the resources necessary to complete projects. Functional managers, typically department managers, by contrast focus on a particular skill or discipline (software engineering, manufacturing, or testing, for example). Functional managers control resources on a continuing basis, meaning their responsibilities generally cross projects where the PMs' responsibility ends with the specific programs or projects to which the PMs are assigned. The scope of a PM can include the development of an entire product line, or it can be limited to a product upgrade or any other activity being uniquely budgeted and tracked. PMs are responsible for creating the budget and schedule to support the completion of uniquely budgeted programs and projects. *What level of control do program or project managers have over budget and schedule?*

The PM function (also referred to as the *program office* in large organizations) is generally implemented through a matrix organization. The PMs draw the resources they need from across the functional departments, for the time they are needed to complete specified tasks. In these organizations, the program office becomes the "customer" of the functional departments. The PMs control the resources, schedule, and fiscal performance of a project. The PMs purchase the labor for the project from the functional departments. The authority of the PMs typically spans the entire life cycle of a project. The life cycle of a project might also include multiple independent subprojects intended to create updated versions or alternate versions of the product. *Is the business structured as a matrix organization?*

Many businesses claim to be matrix organizations, but the roles of the functional managers and the roles of the PMs are performed by the same individuals. For instance, all of the software technical staff report to the software engineering department manager who also has control over the budget and schedule for all of the software development projects. These organizations are not true matrixes, which can indicate that they are person-centric organizations. For businesses with many cross-functional departments, combining these roles doesn't work well (a project might have software, hardware, testing, and support requirements). Therefore, exploring how the business structures its PM and functional management functions will help you understand the business's control structure. Understanding how these functions have been implemented can reveal a potential risk if the PMs see their role as perpetual (projects have an end, even if they are followed by another project) or if the functional managers see their role as temporary. *Does the business separate the roles of functional managers and program or project managers?*

The PMs control projects through the allocation of budgets (in either dollars or hours) to the functional departments. The PMs negotiate the number of hours that will be allocated from the project to each of the functional managers. This provides a cross-check between the functional managers whose focus is in keeping their staff fully employed and the PMs whose focus is in delivering the project within a finite budget. *Do the program or project managers negotiate budgets with the functional managers? Do the program or project managers have responsibility for profits?*

Employee Time Sold

When businesses are structured as matrix organizations, they need to closely manage their employee time sold. When the business charges a project for employee labor hours, the employee time is considered time "sold" and represents a "direct" labor charge; it is billed directly to the project. For instance, if the employee is a database analyst who spends 20 hours per week on one project and 10 hours per week on another, than 30 hours of the employee's time is considered sold. In matrix organizations, the functional managers must attempt to get all of their employee time sold on active projects. In this example, assuming a normal 40 hour workweek, 10 hours of the employee's time is not sold each week. Employee time that is not sold on a project must be charged as indirect time, and it is allocated to a department overhead account that becomes a burden for the employee's home department (and to the overhead of the business as a whole). Vacation time, training time, sick time, and facility closings are all examples of indirect overhead accounts that must be managed by functional managers. It becomes the functional managers' job to control their overhead expenditure rates. *Does the business require functional managers to control their department overhead rates? What indirect accounts does the business track, and are these budgeted?*

In a matrix organization, if the employees' time is not fully sold, the functional managers are responsible for finding additional direct bookings for the employees' time. If the managers cannot do so, the employees' time will be charged to the department overhead or the employees will become part time workers. Some matrix organizations establish minimum time sold standards for each employee (typically 80 to 90 percent). Employees whose time sold falls below the standard are considered at risk if they don't come back above the standard within a short time. This is particularly true if the business is selling employee labor predominantly to government contracts. *Are there any employees identified as at risk due to low time sold?*

Cost Account Management Systems

Most PMs track projects in labor hours rather than dollars. The conversion of labor hours to dollars is performed by the finance group. This allows the functional departments to work with the program office by estimating project tasks in units of labor hours and expenses such as travel. The project office tracks a certain number of people for a certain length of time, eliminating the need for functional managers to deal with labor cost calculations. Other costs, such as material and contract charges, must still be tracked in dollars and eventually rolled up into project costs, allowing the true cost for programs to be tracked and managed by the program office. *Are labor hours converted into dollars and allocated to each project?*

The accounting system is often integrated with a cost account management (CAM) system that is used by the program office to track the actual hours and dollars being charged to the program. *Does the business use a cost account management system to track true project costs?*

The CAM system also includes a mechanism for monitoring the progression of work on a program including the budgeted amount of work accomplished versus the actual amount of work accomplished and the planned schedule versus the actual schedule performance. *Does the CAM system include a mechanism for accurately monitoring the progression of work accomplished on ongoing projects?*

Many businesses fail to track the actual costs involved in developing a product at the time the costs are incurred and instead rely on estimates of the labor hours spent to determine these costs after the project has been completed. Since this type of post-project estimating requires a tremendous amount of subjectivity (and a great memory), the estimates are notoriously inaccurate, and a true cost for developing the product cannot reasonably be determined. Similarly, there may be an opportunity to lower costs if components are reused from one project to another. Spreading the cost for reusable or common code in software product development can lower the overall development expense of a product. *Does the business track and allocate material and contract costs to each project as they are incurred?*

Metrics Collection

The metrics that are tracked through the financial system are a source of valuable data that allow the business to make educated operations decisions. The collection of performance metrics on a continuous basis through an *earned value measurement system* (EVMS) provides an important financial management tool. The extent to which a business relies on its metrics is an indicator of the maturity of the management team. For instance, tracking the trend line showing a history of the ratio between budgeted items—such as the budgeted cost of work performed versus the actual cost of work performed—can indicate whether the managers are metric driven or are making ad hoc operations decisions. "The business has a major project that has completed 80 percent of the schedule but only 50 percent of the work." This type of metric tracking is an indicator of how well the business has estimated past projects, and it can be a direct indictor of potential risks and opportunities. For instance, the trend indicates that the business overestimates development labor so reducing these estimates can be an opportunity to lower prices. Does this indicate that the business has trouble estimating its labor costs or with maintaining its requirements baselines, which could be assessed as a risk? *What performance metrics does the business regularly collect and track?*

Businesses that do extensive work with the government are required to use a certified EVMS. *Does the business use a certified earned value management system (EVMS)?*

Here is another example of a metric commonly used: The difference between a budgeted expense and an actual expense is the *cost variance*, and the difference between projected revenue and actual revenue is the *revenue variance*. These are fundamental relationships that need to be supported by a CAM system that all managers understand and are comfortable working with. The PMs need to be able to explain their program performance in terms of these variances (and functional managers must be able to explain their variances). Your assessment should explore the causes of any significant budget variances. *What do the budget variances indicate about the performance of the business?*

Other metrics trends can be used as risk indicators or for validation of the business's claims. Departments that are expanding, without an equivalent increase in the business's performance, might represent a risk that needs to be explored. While metrics collection has an overhead cost, it provides valuable windows into the operations of the business. Mature businesses recognize this and create automated risk "dashboards" to indicate out-of-tolerance trends based on the data coming from their financial system. If the response of the business is "We don't collect metrics," it may tell you something about the lack of maturity of the management team. *Do the financial metrics indicate if the expenses of each department are going up (or down) in relation to the performance of the business, and is there a reasonable rationale for any variations?*

OPERATIONS REVIEWS

Most businesses hold operations reviews on a monthly basis. Operations reports are generated to support these reviews, and they are used to summarize the performance of the business's operational units for the month (see Figure 10.2). The reviews monitor how well the units are performing against their plan. Operations reviews are typically conducted as part of a management meeting, and they integrate performance metrics on a continuing basis. Operations reviews are one of the ways that managers are

Monthly Operations Report						
	Budget	Actual	Variance	YTD Budget	YTD Actual	YTD Variance
Sales Revenue						
Territory 1	XXXX	XXXX	XXX	XXXXX	XXXXX	XXX
Territory 2	XXXX	XXXX	(XXX)	XXXXX	XXXXX	(XXX)
Territory 3	XXXX	XXXX	XXX	XXXXX	XXXXX	XXX
Total Revenue	XXXX	XXXX	(XXX)	XXXXX	XXXXX	(XXX)
Expenses						
Telephone	(YYYY)	(YYYY)	(YYY)	(YYYYY)	(YYYYY)	(YYY)
Allocated overhead	(YYYY)	(YYYY)	(YYY)	(YYYYY)	(YYYYY)	(YYY)
Salaries	(YYYY)	(YYYY)	(YYY)	(YYYYY)	(YYYYY)	(YYY)
Office expenses	(YYYY)	(YYYY)	(YYY)	(YYYYY)	(YYYYY)	(YYY)
Materials	(YYYY)	(YYYY)	(YYY)	(YYYYY)	(YYYYY)	(YYY)
Total Expenses	(YYYY)	(YYYY)	(YYY)	(YYYYY)	(YYYYY)	(YYY)
Net Earnings	(ZZZZ)	(ZZZZ)	(ZZZ)	(ZZZZZ)	(ZZZZZ)	(ZZZ)

Figure 10.2 A Monthly Operations Report

held accountable for their actions, and they are another indicator of the maturity of the business and its management team. An operations report is a fiscal control tool that is, at a minimum, a combination of the budget and the P&L report. *Does the business hold periodic operations reviews including the preparation of periodic operations reports?*

The operations report provides all of the information managers need to enable them to make near-term tactical decisions about the business's operations. The format for a simple operations report is a compilation of both the budgeted or planned values and the actual values from the P&L report. Many businesses integrate the budget values into their P&L reports, in which case, the P&L report is used as the financial section of the operations report. It needs to present the items that are immediately within the control of the managers.

In many businesses, operations reports are automatically generated from the financial system software. This means that a manager can just give the report a cursory check and then pass it on with little analysis. I advise my clients not to allow this type of token management to occur. Managers should be required to present and explain any significant levels of variance (either plus or minus) in their reports because the variance may indicate real areas of risk or opportunity in time to mitigate the risk or capture the opportunity. *Are managers held accountable for budget and schedule variances, and do they provide a rationale for significant performance deviations?*

Other areas frequently covered by operations reviews include monitoring of staffing reports and sales pipelines. I also like to integrate risk/opportunity management in the operations reports. Managers need to identify their potential operations risks along with their mitigation plans and opportunities along with their capture plans. The risk/opportunity report form provided in Part One offers a good format for this type of reporting. *Are risks and opportunities, along with their mitigation and capture plans, reported by managers on a periodic basis?*

LABOR RATE CALCULATIONS

Determining the full cost of an employee on a per hour basis can be a complex calculation. Labor rate calculation must be done in a manner that allows the business to determine the true billable cost of a project. Does the employee have an office or use electricity? Probably yes. In that case, what portion of the rent or utility bill is allocated to the project along with the employee labor expense? This is determined by calculating a *loaded labor rate* that includes the employee base salary plus the overhead expenses that are allocated to it on a per employee, per hour basis.

Labor rates are a combination of an employee's base salary plus the allocated value of the benefits the employee receives, plus all forms of overhead, such as an allocated portion of the rent, utilities, telephone, and equipment. Add to that the cost of other administrative overheads, such as the cost of management and the result is a fully burdened labor rate for the employee. Tracking expenses by allocating overhead to labor rates in this manner is an important consideration when the business is in a highly competitive market. Lowering the cost of labor therefore is not just a matter of keeping salaries down. It is also a matter of managing the business's overhead expenses. You will learn a lot by going through the makeup of the labor rates, including direct and indirect costs, as a means of determining how the business's overhead structure is impacting its cost of doing business. Could the overhead rates be changed, creating an opportunity to make the business more competitive, by moving to a different facility or changing benefit plans? *Does the business track its loaded labor rates? Can the business provide a breakdown of its loaded labor rates?*

PRODUCT WARRANTEES AND GUARANTEES

Warrantees and guarantees on products can represent a tremendous hidden cost for a business and a potential risk for an investor. Product warrantees and guarantees can lead to unplanned recurring expenses that are often not disclosed or evident in the financial forecasts. You will need to explore the types of product warrantees and guarantees that have been issued for which there are still outstanding liabilities. You will also need to determine if the warrantees and guarantees planned for the future are consistent with past expenses and whether or not they have been adequately planned for the future. *Does the business's budget include the cost for warranty repairs?*

Sustainable businesses track the offsetting relationship ensuring that the cost for quality assurance (such as product testing) of its products outweighs the cost for repairs. They also monitor the market impact of quality on the reputation of the business. *What is the history of warranty payments or reimbursements for product guarantees?*

If there are any known product defects that have not been previously repaired, then the cost for these repairs needs to be budgeted and the impact of these repairs on operations must be planned. For instance, if the development staff is required to make the repairs, is this the same staff that is responsible for ongoing development? If so, there might be a risk that the repairs will impact the schedules and delivery of new products. The impact of extending development activities to support repairs has to be planned. *Are there any pending or suspected customer claims based on known product defects?*

PRESCHEDULED GROWTH

There are often areas where a business has had a history of cost growth, such as annual increases in payroll and benefits, which have become accepted as the norm for the business and where cost growth can become "scheduled in" without realizing it. These operating cost expansions can represent a significant risk if they haven't been identified during due diligence or included in future plans. Changing these norms can create significant employee problems. "But we always receive a 5 percent raise." These are scheduled-in expansions that can impact the business's expense burn rate, and they should be anticipated (but might not be pointed out during due diligence).

Such prescheduled cost expansions may not be optional if they are buried in things like contingencies tied to employee offer letters or informal, undocumented agreements based on an accepted, but unpublished, growth formula. In either case, there should be a clear disclosure of any scheduled cost growth that will occur. Profit sharing plans that have "always been offered" but are not documented with guarantees should be clearly understood and disclosed. *Have all scheduled cost increases been identified and disclosed?*

EMPLOYEE OWNERSHIP AND OPTIONS

Another area of concern, particularly in small businesses, is the handling of employee option plans. Start-up businesses tend to hand out options easily as a means of attracting top talent. As the business grows and the staff changes, these businesses are notorious for losing track of what options they have issued or promised. The result is a potential for stock dilution to occur without being accurately tracked. As an investor, you will require a clear statement of outstanding ownership. There is a risk that some key employees will become disenfranchised if they find the verbal agreements they thought they had have not been identified.

The question of ownership goes to the spirit and culture of many businesses and often includes some levels of employee participation. Employee-owned businesses, called *employee stock ownership plans* (ESOPs), are formed on the belief that employee ownership will result in greater employee motivation. Many businesses are not ESOP businesses but they are still generous when handing out stock options. Again, this is common in early stage businesses. You should be aware of this and expect an accounting of which employees hold options and how many options have been issued or promised by the business. *Is the employee option plan accounted for within the growth provisions of the business, and will the employee-owned stocks cause stock dilution? How many outstanding employee options are there, and under what terms were they issued (e.g., term, value, or vesting)?*

BANKING

Part of the day-to-day operations of any business includes its banking relationships. Understanding the nature of these relationships can give you a lot of information about the ability of the business to sustain its operations. This relationship includes the ability of the business to access credit when needed. *What is the status of the business's banking relationships?*

Overdrawn accounts and late payments on loans indicate a struggling business and therefore a potentially high-risk investment. Stable businesses tend to retain the same banks for long periods of time while businesses that are struggling financially tend to change banks often. *How stable have the business's banking relationships been, and what were the reasons for any recent changes?*

Although usually the cash needs of businesses are relatively predictable, it is sometimes difficult to predict the ups and downs of sales or the fluctuations of the market. The result, even for stable businesses, can be a shortfall in the cash they require to support their near-term operations. Most businesses establish a line of credit with their bank to help them meet their short-term cash needs. Exploring the way a business utilizes its lines of credit reveals a lot about the health of that business. *What lines of credit does the business have, and what is the history of its use of those funds?*

Summary of the Financial Infrastructure Questions

1. Does each manager have a defined and documented level of financial signature authority?
2. Who is the senior financial officer of the business?
3. Is there a written policy that defines the rules for financial commitment of the business?
4. Does the business need to comply with the Sarbanes-Oxley Act, or does it anticipate a future compliance requirement?
5. How does the business enforce the collection and archiving of Sarbanes-Oxley compliant data?
6. What is the cost for retention and archiving of Sarbanes-Oxley compliant data and reports?
7. How does the business audit its Sarbanes-Oxley compliance?
8. Has the accuracy of the business's financial reports been validated?
9. Do the prior tax returns support the business's income and expense claims?
10. Do all group managers review their P&L reports on a periodic basis?
11. Do the revenue, expense, or earnings trends reflected in the P&L reports indicate any operational risks or opportunities?
12. Does the balance sheet identify any operational risks or opportunities for the business?
13. Have the cash reserves dwindled over time?
14. Has the business established a track record for timely collection of its accounts receivable?
15. Has the business established a track record for meeting its accounts payable obligations on time?

16. Has the business failed to make any of its past payroll expenses in a timely manner?
17. Are cash flow statements regularly used to predict operational cash needs?
18. Are revenue projections available for at least the next three years?
19. How much detail is behind the business's pro forma projections?
20. Does the business track the time-to-market for each product line?
21. If the projections show hockey stick growth, is there a rationale to support this increase, and is there an equivalent ramp-up in the operations expenses of the business?
22. Is the marketing lead flow sufficient to support the projected revenues?
23. Is the business reporting all sales and all operating expenses, or is it making pro forma adjustments?
24. Are budgets created at each operational level of the organization?
25. Are budgets created using historic records of prior expenses?
26. Do functional managers own their budgets, or does finance create their budgets for them?
27. Is financial authority delegated to all managers to execute their operations plan according to their approved budget?
28. How are budget performance goals established?
29. Do managers document their budget assumptions?
30. Is there a mechanism for modifying the budget in response to the changing operational needs of the business?
31. Does the business hold a management reserve?
32. What level of control do program or project managers have over budget and schedule?
33. Is the business structured as a matrix organization?
34. Does the business separate the roles of functional managers and program or project managers?
35. Do the program or project managers negotiate budgets with the functional managers?
36. Do program or project managers have responsibility for profits?
37. Does the business require functional managers to control their department overhead rates?
38. What indirect accounts does the business track, and are these budgeted?

39. Are there any employees identified as at risk due to low time sold?
40. Are labor hours converted into dollars and allocated to each project?
41. Does the business use a cost account management system to track true project costs?
42. Does the CAM system include a mechanism for accurately monitoring the progression of work accomplished on ongoing projects?
43. Does the business track and allocate material and contract costs to each project as they are incurred?
44. What performance metrics does the business regularly collect and track?
45. Does the business use a certified earned value measurement system (EVMS)?
46. What do the budget variances indicate about the performance of the business?
47. Do the financial metrics indicate if the expenses of each department are going up (or down) in relation to the performance of the business, and is there reasonable rationale for any variations?
48. Does the business hold periodic operations reviews including the preparation of periodic operations reports?
49. Are managers held accountable for budget and schedule variances, and do they provide a rationale for significant performance deviations?
50. Are risks and opportunities, along with their mitigation and capture plans, reported by management on a periodic basis?
51. Does the business track its loaded labor rates? Can the business provide a breakdown of its loaded labor rates?
52. Does the business's budget include the cost for warranty repairs?
53. What is the history of warranty payments or reimbursements for product guarantees?
54. Are there any pending or suspected customer claims based on known product defects?
55. Have all scheduled cost increases been identified and disclosed?
56. Is the employee option plan accounted for within the growth provisions of the business, and will the employee-owned stocks cause dilution?

57. How many outstanding employee options are there, and under what terms were they issued (e.g., term, value, or vesting)?
58. What is the status of the business's banking relationships?
59. How stable have the business's banking relationships been, and what were the reasons for any recent changes?
60. What lines of credit does the business have, and what is the history of its use of those funds?

CHAPTER 11

Assessment of the Legal Infrastructure

By 1866, the U.S. railroads had grown and extended their reach throughout the country as far as the Pacific. The large railroad businesses were the modern technology businesses of their time. In order to protect their railbeds, the railroads often lined their tracks with fences that spanned hundreds of miles. The state of California, looking for additional sources of revenue, began assessing taxes on property owned by the railroads including placing taxes on these fences that were assessed on a per mile basis. The taxes quickly became a tremendous burden on the railroads. It seems that placing large taxes on businesses is a well-established legacy in California!

These taxes were assessed on the railroads at the full value of the fenced properties and on the fences themselves rather than at the discount rate that was being given to individual property owners. The railroads started to resist paying taxes on their fences, and in 1886, Santa Clara County and the state of California ended up in court with the Southern Pacific Railroad. The railroad argued that the county did not have jurisdiction over the areas where these fences were, based on a technicality in the law. The case made its way to the U.S. Supreme Court, which eventually found in favor of the railroad (U.S. Supreme Court Reports, *Santa Clara County v. Southern Pacific Railroad*, 118 U.S. 394, 1886).

The notable part of this story, however, is the declaration made by Chief Justice Waite about the nature of a corporation. Chief Justice Waite made the following declaration prior to hearing arguments in the case: "The court does not wish to hear argument on the question of whether the provision in the Fourteenth Amendment to the Constitution, which forbids a State to deny to any person within its jurisdiction the equal protection of the laws, applies to these corporations. . . . We are all of the opinion that it does." The Fourteenth Amendment guarantees all citizens equal justice under the law. The decision meant that individuals and corporations were equal in the eyes of the law. With this statement, corporations gained the recognition and status of individuals under the U.S. Constitution. There are obvious limitations and controls on businesses, however. For instance, corporations don't vote, and there are many other limitations placed on them. The importance of this case was that the Supreme Court of the United States defined the nature of a business. As a result, corporations were given a legal persona.

While a business enjoys the legal status of an individual, it is in fact a legal entity that relies on the coordinated actions of many individuals. How do you coordinate the actions of many individuals to ensure that all of their actions are conducted in an ethical, honest, and legal manner, on a continuous basis? The legal infrastructure provides the framework necessary to guide and control the continuing legal operations of the business. When assessing the legal infrastructure, more than any other operations area, identifying the weakest link in this framework is critical. By violating the rules, one person or act could potentially destroy the business. Also, businesses can operate across a very wide range of geographic, demographic, and market environments, each of which potentially requires compliance with established local, state, federal, and international laws. *Does the business have documented policies and procedures that guide its legal operations?*

The legal infrastructure is the framework that guides the legal operations of a business on a continuing basis. It includes all of the policies, procedures, and other activities used to protect the business from legal risks and liabilities.

Operations Due Diligence of the legal infrastructure is an assessment of the ongoing legal operations of the business. As with financial due diligence, there is a distinct difference between legal due diligence and Operations Due Diligence of the legal infrastructure. Legal due diligence is an assessment of the current legal status of the business, and it is not covered here. Legal due diligence is the domain of attorneys and is performed to assess the current legal status of the business. It is used to determine if the business has any existing or pending legal liabilities.

While performing an operations assessment, you may also find clues to help discover the cause of any legacy liability resulting from past actions by the business. If there were problems, why did they occur, and what is protecting the business from repeating these mistakes in the future? Legal due diligence and Operations Due Diligence of the legal infrastructure are mutually supportive. Both legal due diligence and Operations Due

Diligence of the legal infrastructure are required to protect you from potential risk. Legal due diligence assesses the business at a point in time. It ensures that, at the closing, the business is free and clear of any liability that could pass to the investors, that there are no outstanding or pending legal actions against the business, and that there are no legal obstacles that would limit the ability of the business to continue to operate.

All M&A events, and major investment actions of any kind, require support from a qualified attorney. Attorneys play several important roles in these transactions including overseeing the legal due diligence, preparing the legal transfer of the title, reviewing any existing contracts or agreements, and finally executing the closing. Nothing in this section is meant to replace or reduce the need for a full legal due diligence assessment conducted by a qualified attorney.

> Nothing in this section is meant to replace or reduce the need for a full legal due diligence assessment conducted by a qualified attorney.

An assessment of the continuing legal operations of the business is required to identify and mitigate future legal risk and liability. How do you know, for instance, if safeguards exist to prevent the business from executing a bad agreement immediately following the closing? Protections may need to be put in place prior to the closing to ensure that there is no disruption of the business. Is the business license still valid? Or are the professional certifications the business carries still current? It's easy to think of the legal infrastructure in terms of risk mitigation, such as limiting liability that could result in litigation, but Operations Due Diligence is the place to explore opportunities such as identifying latent intellectual property that may not have been previously identified, captured, or protected through patents, copyrights, or trademarks.

Operations deficiencies will be identified during the legal due diligence (such as poorly executed agreements that are difficult to novate), and the reasons for this type of deficiency need to become targets for further exploration during the Operations Due Diligence. Why did management execute bad agreements in the past? How were they reviewed? Who was authorized to sign them? The business needs to have a legal infrastructure in place that protects its owners and its assets throughout all of its operations. Operations Due Diligence explores how the business makes legal commitments in all of its contracts and agreements, who is allowed to make binding commitments, and how the business legally protects its capital and proprietary assets.

The legal infrastructure has to integrate a set of checks and balances that control and monitor the legal operations of the business and ensure its lawful operation at all times. To accomplish this, the legal infrastructure must be institutionalized and enforced through enforced policies and procedures that are reviewed and updated on a regular basis. *Does the business review its legal policies and procedures on at least an annual basis?*

While striving to reach a high level of perfection in ethical, honest, and legal matters, it's clear that this may not be achieved, and protections must be built into the infrastructure to protect the business from legal liability and risk. Often, the only legal defense a business has when employees violate the rules is to demonstrate that the individuals acted on their own, without authorization, and went outside the enforced policies and procedures of the business when committing a violation. The business needs to show that its resulting actions were direct and were taken immediately to resolve any issues, as soon as they were recognized. And of course, having a documented legal infrastructure to back up this claim and demonstrating a willingness to take the appropriate actions when a violation does occur is also necessary. *Does the business have a reputation for ethical, honest, and legal operations?*

CONTRACTS, AGREEMENTS, AND OTHER BINDING DOCUMENTS

Businesses enter into many forms of binding documents as part of their ongoing operations. These include purchase agreements, sales agreements, nondisclosure agreements, real estate or lease agreements, development contracts, employee offer letters, labor negotiations, and on and on. All documents that legally bind the business or that stipulate terms between the business and another party need to be treated as contracts, and they are considered binding commitments by the business.

There are legally defined criteria, such as mutual consent, that must be met for a document to meet the definition of a legally binding document. This is a good discussion for you to have with your attorney! In some instances, this can also include public statements by the business or its employees that can be implied as commitments (such as advertising or verbal statements by managers). Ideally, of course, all legal commitments will be reviewed by an attorney and signed by the CEO. Realistically, this won't be the case for most businesses, and even a very large public corporation with a permanent staff of inside counsel might find these practices costly and inefficient. *How does the business manage its legal agreements and binding documents?*

One way to efficiently manage binding documents is to standardize the document templates into forms and to conduct a legal review of the templates prior to their use. This works for frequently used documents such as employee offer letters, nondisclosure agreements, contractor agreements, and any other documents that are used many times over. The procedures for using these documents also need to be published, and they should include alternate procedures to use when the other party asks to have the standard modified. *Does the business have standard templates for recurring documents, and have those templates had a complete legal review?*

Binding documents that cannot be standardized need to be reviewed individually. Determining how and when these reviews are accomplished and who conducts the reviews need to be defined by policy. It may not be cost effective or efficient to send all documents to an attorney for review. Whenever a binding document is issued without being reviewed by an attorney, the business is deciding to make a commitment and accept some level of risk. Most businesses allow a management review that the business considers acceptable as an alternate to review by an attorney. The managers need to recognize that they are signing a binding document that has a potential liability and that they are committing the future actions of the business in some manner. When making a decision to bind the business in a way that could incur risk, an assessment of the risk should be performed. *Does the business allow some level of management sign-off on binding documents without review by an attorney?*

LEGAL SIGNATURE AUTHORITY

The ability of individuals to make binding legal commitments for the business needs to be carefully controlled. Individuals who have this authorization must be clearly identified. When executing binding documents, a two-step process needs to be used. The first step is the review of the document by a person with the skills to perform a subject review, and the second step is the actual signing of the document by a person with the authority to do so. These steps can be accomplished by two separate individuals, but legal signature authority is required for step 2. Managers who have the authority to perform step 2 need to understand that step 1 should never be skipped.

Legal signature authority is often combined with financial signature authority because they're typically delegated to the same individuals. These authorities aren't the same, however, and they need to be treated differently. Financial commitment has an immediate measurable impact on the business (authorization to purchase a budgeted service, for instance). Legal commitment, on the other hand, is more often tied to longer-term potential impacts on the business (a future violation of a particular agreement could have an effect years from now), the cost of which can't be determined. Financial operations are constrained by a budget whereas legal operations tend to be far more subjective.

Since many businesses fail to make a distinction between legal and financial authority, many managers don't take the time to consider the difference. A manager may have the financial authority to execute an agreement that commits the business to spend $50,000, and the manager may be willing to do this if he or she has a sufficient budget and the financial authority to make this commitment. The agreement might also have terms that create a significant legal liability for the business that goes far beyond this amount. Because the manager has the financial authority does not mean that he or she is authorized to make the legal commitment. Clear delineation and allocation of both the legal and financial authority are necessary. *Does the business make a distinction between financial signature authority and legal signature authority?*

Many times, I find that managers are not able to clearly explain their authority to make legal commitments for the business because there are no published guidelines for them to follow. Then, when a problem does occur, the explanation I hear given by the business usually goes something like this: "We pay managers to make good decisions. He should have known better than to sign that." True, he may have shown poor judgment, but the business cannot abdicate its responsibility to be clear in describing the nature of the authority it is delegating to its managers.

The next thing the manager may hear in this scenario is that he is being terminated for signing an agreement that ended in litigation. All managers need to receive a definition of their authority to commit the business, and more important, all managers should ask for this authority in writing before signing any document. *How does the business delegate legal signature authority?*

Many businesses incorporate a contracts group into their legal infrastructure. The contracts department is staffed with contract specialists and paralegals who are able to understand and interpret the complex legal language used in contracts (particularly government contracts). The contracts group works closely with inside counsel and occasionally is in the same department. Generally, the contracts group is an inbound function. The group's role is to parse all contractual requirements to ensure that the business is in compliance with the terms of the contracts and meeting its commitments. Because of the paralegal nature of the contracts group, some businesses assign the responsibility for first-level review of binding documents to the contracts group rather than relying solely on the judgment of individual managers. *Does the business have a contracts group?*

GOVERNMENT CONTRACTS

Government agencies require businesses to comply with a large number of regulations in order to qualify for a contract. Federal, state, and local governments all incorporate regulations into their contracts that are intended to implement public policy as well as control the cost and the quality of the actual products delivered. The federal government, for instance, integrates a set of regulations known as Federal Acquisition Regulations (FARs) into their contracts. The imposition of federal regulations can significantly increase the scope of the contract terms and is the cause of excessive prices for government-purchased products. Consider the following example: The "Table of HR Policies" is an example of the regulations that the federal government incorporates into its contracts that direct how a business will manage its human resources (HR) under the contract. The federal regulations listed in the "Table of HR Policies" are subject to change over time, and most likely there will be policies added to it. The cost impact to implement each of these regulations is added to the price the business charges for its products.

Table of HR Policies

Americans with Disabilities Act
Age Discrimination Act
Family and Medical Leave Act
Civil Rights Acts
Immigration Reform and Control Act
Fair Credit Reporting Act
Drug Free Workplace Act
National Labor Relations Act
Jury System Improvement Act
Uniformed Services Employment Act
Polygraph Protection Act

Ensuring that the business has accounted for all of the regulations listed here that the government imposes on it is an important operations risk assessment.

- *How does the business comply with the intent of the Americans with Disabilities Act?*
- *How does the business comply with the intent of the Age Discrimination Act?*
- *How does the business comply with the intent of the Family and Medical Leave Act?*
- *How does the business comply with the intent of the Civil Rights Acts?*
- *How does the business comply with the intent of the Immigration Reform and Control Act?*
- *How does the business comply with the intent of the Fair Credit Reporting Act?*
- *How does the business comply with the intent of the Drug Free Workplace Act?*
- *How does the business comply with the intent of the National Labor Relations Act?*
- *How does the business comply with the intent of the Jury System Improvement Act?*

- *How does the business comply with the intent of the Uniformed Services Employment Act?*
- *How does the business comply with the intent of the Polygraph Protection Act?*

Careful reading of all of the terms of a government contract is required to ensure that the business is in compliance and has accounted for the cost of implementing these regulations in its pricing. Because a violation of these regulations can result in the loss of contracts and high potential fines, a significant risk exists when a business fails to integrate them into its operations. *How does the business ensure compliance with government contract regulations?*

Similar regulations exist in all countries and all levels of government. The specific regulations may change, but the need to comply is a requirement for doing business with the government.

Any business entering into a contract with the government must carefully review and comply with all of the terms of the contract. Your assessment should include parsing the terms of all active government contracts. Some of these requirements can have extensive cost and operations implications.

Since many of these government regulations deal with the historic records of the business, if a business plans on doing government contract work in the future, it should research the requirements for these contracts, and it should plan in advance how it will comply, including how it will collect and store the data needed to demonstrate its compliance. *Is the business currently a government contractor, or is it planning on future business with the government?*

COMPLIANCE

Compliance with all the rules and regulations that regulate businesses can be a tremendous obstacle that can seem insurmountable. The problem isn't just dealing with existing regulations. Many times these regulations continue to evolve and can impact the strategic direction of the business over night. The business needs a process for continuously monitoring its compliance with evolving regulations that could change either its operations or the market it sells into. This process needs to constantly identify and assess the impact of changing regulations and establish strategies to remain compliant with them.

These regulations are imposed by multiple federal, state, and local agencies. For instance, states impose regulations on businesses such as professional and business licensing, and local governments impose regulations such as operating permits. *Does the business have all of the professional licenses it requires?*

Failure to comply with government regulations can be expensive, resulting in fines or complete suspension of operations. Conducting a periodic compliance review can help to mitigate the risk of a violation. *How does the business review and monitor the rules and regulations that govern its operations?*

Government regulations are often complex and require specialists to interpret and implement. One way to mitigate the risk posed by changing regulations is to employ specialists to advise the business on these changes. These specialists can be outside consultants familiar with these specific regulations or full-time employees when the expense is justifiable. The cost for these resources is often overlooked in the budget. *Does the business employ specialists, such as financial and market consultants, to help it comply with complex and/or changing regulations?*

INTELLECTUAL PROPERTY

The creative work efforts of a business result in proprietary assets, including unique product designs and technologies, manufacturing methods, white papers, brand designs, and logos, which all become the intellectual property of the business. These intellectual property assets bring value to the business and need to be protected by patents, trademarks, or copyrights.

There are many cases in which businesses have developed some great new product idea, they then pay to produce it and advertise it, and then they are surprised a short while later when their competition starts advertising a similar product (often for less since the competition was able to copy theirs rather than pay to develop its own). These businesses may have been avoiding the initial cost for filing a patent, trademark, or copyright to protect their assets, but in the end they paid a much greater price from the competitive loss and the lost opportunity to add a valuable asset to their business. *What intellectual property has the business identified and captured in the form of patents, trademarks, or copyrights?*

Businesses frequently create intellectual property but fail to recognize it as such and therefore fail to capture and protect it legally. In many cases, the employees have just never been trained to know what intellectual property is or how to identify it. In technology businesses, technical staff members in particular need to be trained to recognize intellectual property, and they should be given incentives to identify it. Because of the value intellectual property can bring, many businesses incorporate an incentive plan to encourage employees to identify, create, and capture intellectual property. *Are employees trained to recognize and identify intellectual property?*

Copies of the existing intellectual property documentation are generally reviewed as part of the legal due diligence. In conducting a due diligence of the legal infrastructure, however, a search for potential intellectual property is also helpful in identifying where other latent intellectual property might exist that was not previously captured. A good place to start your search is to look for products that the business considers proprietary and that it relies on for its sales or operations, but are products for which there has been no attempt to capture as intellectual property. This is a great place to ask, Why not? Identifying new intellectual property would mean that the business has been undervalued, which could be a major opportunity discovery. You need to determine why these assets were not identified as intellectual property in the past. If they really are proprietary, why weren't they protected?

Since intellectual property assets add value to the business, there will be a tendency to overstate their value and status to potential investors. The BS Quotient can definitely come into play here. This is another area where a distinction needs to be made between the goals of legal due diligence and the goals of Operations Due Diligence. Legal due diligence will establish the status of any existing intellectual property and deal with any assignment issues, such as patents that are listed as pending. Operations Due Diligence is concerned with the value, content, and completeness of the captured intellectual property and the continuing process to bring these about. *Is the existing intellectual property protection sufficient to protect the proprietary assets of the business?*

Along with protecting their own intellectual property, businesses must be constantly diligent that they don't violate someone else's intellectual property. It's not unusual for many people to come up with the same idea. During the research and development phase of a product's life cycle, the business needs to perform searches to identify potential conflicts. These searches are much easier to conduct today through the use of the Internet. When a conflict is discovered, the business must stop or modify its approach or license the use of the intellectual property from its rightful owner. Intellectual property infringement can be very costly. *Does the business have any potential intellectual property infringements?*

You will need to have searches done if there are any concerns in this area. When intellectual property is licensed, there are usually restrictions on how that intellectual property may be assigned or used by another party. During an acquisition, for instance, these licenses may have to be assigned to the new owners. *Has all intellectual property on which the business depends been identified, and will it need to be reassigned following an acquisition?*

INSURANCE

Risk avoidance is a requirement in the day-to-day operations of any business. Insurance is expensive, but all businesses must protect their operations, assets, employees, and owners. The type of insurance a business must carry depends on its operations and the market it is in. As a minimum, it needs to include protection from the common risks such as legal liability, fire, and theft. It may also include coverage such as specialized malpractice insurance, director's liability insurance, and errors and omissions insurance. As a business grows, the types and limits of its insurance will change. There needs to be an annual review of the types and amounts of coverage that are needed. *Does the business have sufficient insurance coverage, and does it review its coverage on an annual basis?*

Looking at past insurance claims may also be an indicator of the business's past operations and risks. Have there been prior claims for stolen property or health issues? *What outstanding insurance claims are there, and what claims has the business filed in the past?*

DOCUMENT RETENTION POLICY

All *electronically stored information* (ESI) is subject to the federal rules of evidence and must be preserved in its native form if a subpoena is issued or if one is anticipated.

The Federal Rules of Civil Procedure (FRCP) defines how evidence is used in civil legal proceedings. The FRCP now makes all electronically stored business documents (including employee e-mail, spreadsheets, and working papers), known as *electronically stored information* (ESI), admissible as evidence in legal actions. All forms of electronically stored information are subject to the FRCP. Employees who perform work from home, on their own computers, may also be subject to having the hard drives on their personal computers subpoenaed. Because of these rules, all businesses should implement and follow a document retention policy that clearly states which documents must be saved and for how long, and how to determine when these documents can be destroyed or deleted. *Does the business have a document retention policy, and is there evidence that the policy is being enforced?*

Subpoenaing of documents and records, including employee e-mail, has become a common litigation practice today. This practice is known as *electronic data discovery* (EDD). ESI records, including backup tapes and online archives, that have been subpoenaed, or for which there is a reasonable expectation that they will be subpoenaed in the future, may not be modified, deleted, or destroyed. Furthermore, they are subject to a data hold (a *data hold* means that, if the document is scheduled for destruction, it may not be, and it must continue to be retained).

Most ESI also contains hidden data known as *metadata*. Metadata is information about the electronic document that is stored within hidden file layers when the document is created or modified. It can include items such as the author and the creation and modification dates, and it is hidden unless the user has the tools to extract and view it. If the ESI is subject to a data hold order, the metadata must also be preserved along with the document. All employees need to be made aware that all documents, including their personal e-mail sent from a work computer, belong to the business and any deleted, edited, or revised electronic documents can be recovered and restored using modern electronic data discovery techniques. *Does the document retention policy address ESI that is subject to a data hold?*

PRIVACY PROTECTION

In 2007 the Federal Trade Commission (FTC) took action against the American United Mortgage Company for an offense that took place in 2005 in violation of the Fair and Accurate Credit Transactions Act (FACTA).

The complaint asserted that the business had disposed of personal information by leaving intact hundreds of documents in a nearby unsecured dumpster, in some cases in open trash bags. According to the FTC's complaint, "American United collects personal information about consumers, including Social Security numbers, bank and credit card account numbers, income and credit histories, and consumer reports. Among other things, the company allegedly failed to implement reasonable policies and procedures requiring the proper disposal of consumers' personal information, including consumer reports; to take reasonable actions in disposing of such information; and to identify reasonably foreseeable internal and external risks to consumer information." The company also allegedly failed to develop, implement, or maintain a comprehensive written information security program.

The complaint charged American United Mortgage Company with violating the FTC's Disposal Rule, which requires companies to dispose of credit reports and information from credit reports "in a safe and appropriate manner," and the FTC's Safeguards Rule, which requires financial institutions to take appropriate measures to protect their customer information.

The American United Mortgage Corporation agreed to pay a $50,000 fine for failing to implement reasonable safeguards to protect customer information and failing to provide customers with privacy notices.

The founders of the U.S. Constitution were very concerned about the invasion of privacy of individuals, and therefore, they provided protections that guaranteed the rights of individuals to privacy from the government. The founders of the United States, however, never envisioned the need to protect the rights of personal privacy between one citizen and another. The possession of personal data, such as Social Security numbers, health-care records, driver's license numbers, and other data about individuals is a common requirement for the operation of many businesses. Businesses often possess personal data for their employees, customer records, and other third-party personal data, and they may handle this data in the normal course of doing business. There are a number of statutes and regulations that protect the rights of individuals to have their personal data protected. *What personal data does the business possess that is covered by privacy rules and/or regulations? Is the business aware of all privacy regulations that apply to its operational data?*

All personal information in the possession of a business must be properly protected and disposed of. Disposal includes any discarding, abandonment, sale, donation, or transfer of the information. Special care should be taken when disposing of old computers, with intact hard drives that contain private data (even if it has been deleted), to make sure the data is fully destroyed by physically destroying the hard drive. *How does the business dispose of personal confidential information that it has in its possession?*

The theft of personal identities has become one of the leading high-tech crimes of the twenty-first century. The federal government and most state governments have now passed laws that deal with breaches of the personal information used to commit these crimes. These laws provide stiff penalties and requirements for the notification of individuals when a breach of their data has occurred. The rules are often industry dependent and can be a large burden for some businesses.

Along with the use of this data comes a tremendous liability for the business to protect the data from disclosure outside of the business. Businesses these days are under constant attack by intruders trying to gain access to personal data that is under the businesses' control. *What steps has the business taken to protect and monitor access to its employee, customer, and third-party privacy data?*

Summary of the Legal Infrastructure Questions

1. Does the business have documented policies and procedures that guide its legal operations?
2. Does the business review its legal policies and procedures on at least an annual basis?
3. Does the business have a reputation for ethical, honest, and legal operations?
4. How does the business manage its legal agreements and binding documents?
5. Does the business have standard templates for recurring documents, and have those templates had a complete legal review?
6. Does the business allow some level of management sign-off on binding documents without review by an attorney?
7. Does the business make a distinction between financial signature authority and legal signature authority?

8. How does the business delegate legal signature authority?
9. Does the business have a contracts group?
10. How does the business comply with the intent of the Americans with Disabilities Act?
11. How does the business comply with the intent of the Age Discrimination Act?
12. How does the business comply with the intent of the Family and Medical Leave Act?
13. How does the business comply with the intent of the Civil Rights Acts?
14. How does the business comply with the intent of the Immigration Reform and Control Act?
15. How does the business comply with the intent of the Fair Credit Reporting Act?
16. How does the business comply with the intent of the Drug Free Workplace Act?
17. How does the business comply with the intent of the National Labor Relations Act?
18. How does the business comply with the intent of the Jury System Improvement Act?
19. How does the business comply with the intent of the Uniformed Services Employment Act?
20. How does the business comply with the intent of the Polygraph Protection Act?
21. How does the business ensure compliance with government contract regulations?
22. Is the business currently a government contractor, or is it planning on future business with the government?
23. Have the requirements for professional licensing changed recently and does that effect the businesses operations?
24. Does the business have all of the professional licenses it requires?
25. How does the business review and monitor the rules and regulations that govern its operations?
26. Does the business employ specialists, such as financial and market consultants, to help it comply with complex and/or changing regulations?
27. What intellectual property has the business identified and captured in the form of patents, trademarks, or copyrights?

28. Are employees trained to recognize and identify intellectual property?
29. Is the existing intellectual property protection sufficient to protect the proprietary assets of the business?
30. Does the business have any potential intellectual property infringements?
31. Has all intellectual property on which the business depends been identified, and will it need to be reassigned following an acquisition?
32. Does the business have sufficient insurance coverage, and does it review its coverage on an annual basis?
33. What outstanding insurance claims are there, and what claims has the business filed in the past?
34. Does the business have a document retention policy, and is there evidence that the policy is being enforced?
35. Does the document retention policy address ESI that is subject to a data hold?
36. What personal data does the business possess that is covered by privacy rules and/or regulations?
37. Is the business aware of all privacy regulations that apply to its operational data?
38. How does the business dispose of personal confidential information that it has in its possession?
39. What steps has the business taken to protect and monitor access to its employee, customer, and third-party privacy data?

CHAPTER 12

Assessment of the Institutionalized Processes

In 1901 Henry Ford (along with a group of investors) founded the Henry Ford Company. Ford soon became dissatisfied with this business, however, because it didn't reflect his personal interest, which was to build automobiles that the average American could afford to own. He eventually sold his shares and left the business. After Ford left the Henry Ford Company, the business was renamed as the Cadillac Automobile Company.

In 1903, with $28,000 from a second group of investors, Henry Ford established the Ford Motor Company. The Ford Motor Company instituted an assembly line process, allowing the company to mass produce automobiles, which kept production costs low and allowed Ford to achieve his goals for building an inexpensive automobile. The Ford Motor Company became the first automobile manufacturer to institutionalize the use of a mass production process.

While Henry Ford is often referred to as the "father of the automobile," what he actually invented was not the automobile (others had done this before him). Rather, he applied the principles of mass production through the use of interchangeable parts to the manufacture of automobiles, making the automobile affordable for most families. The family that bought a Ford automobile knew exactly what they were getting, and they also knew that, if it broke, they could find replacement parts to repair it. The days of the one-of-a-kind automobile were gone. Using a mass production process meant that replaceable parts had to be used in the production process. It also meant that the cost of the product could be managed by constantly improving the production process. By focusing on its production processes, Ford created a sustainable business built on an efficient and constantly improving infrastructure.

A business that invests the resources to improve its operations infrastructure will become more efficient, making it more competitive, improving its profits, and therefore making it more sustainable.

Unfortunately, there are many businesses that still don't seem to understand the benefits and importance of institutionalizing their processes. They resist committing the resources to conduct a continuous process improvement program. As a result, many of these businesses' processes become one-of-a-kind solutions. Each new project becomes a unique experience because the businesses aren't following an institutionalized process or set of standards. Consequently, they continually encounter risks, performing similar tasks differently each time and missing the opportunity to improve their operations over time. The end result is often poor quality and lower profits, missed schedules, and blown cost estimates. They are returning to the methods that were common prior to 1903! *Does the business operate in an ad hoc manner, or does it operate in a determined, focused manner that it constantly seeks to improve?*

The methods and processes a business chooses to institutionalize become a driver for its competitiveness, product quality, and cost of doing business. The business's institutionalized processes also become part of the culture and character of the business. Process management, therefore, should be endemic to the way a business conducts its operations. *Does the business routinely document its operational policies and procedures, and is there evidence that employees are following them?*

> Process management should be endemic to the way a business conducts its operations.

Unlike the other chapters in *Operations Due Diligence*, this chapter crosses all of the infrastructure areas rather than focusing on any one area.

There are a number of standardized process methodologies that can be used to institutionalize a business's operations. These methods have been developed by independent industry certification organizations, and they are used to establish standards for practitioners in their industries. Some of the more popular methods include ISO 9001, CMM/CMMI (ISO/IEC 15504), Six Sigma, total quality management (TQM), and Lean Manufacturing.

Determining which method a business will adopt is very much market and product driven. Determining which method will be institutionalized is very much dependent on the type of business and the market it is selling into. Government software contracts often require CMM/CMMI certification, for instance, and international product sales often require ISO 9001 certification. By institutionalizing one of these methods, the business is choosing to formalize its operations infrastructure according to established industry standards, and it is committing resources to the implementation of its operations infrastructure.

In November 2009 the International Standards Organization (ISO) released a new family of risk management standards. The use of these standards quickly gained traction in Japan and in the United Kingdom, and they slowly began to get attention in the United States under the leadership of the American Society of Safety Engineers (ASSE). This family of standards includes ISO/IEC 73 (Risk Management Vocabulary), ISO 31000:2009 (Principles and Guidelines on Implementation), and ISO 31010:2010 (Risk Management–Risk Assessment Techniques). Institutionalizing the methods described by these standards has great potential because they will create a risk management framework for a business. The adoption of these standards as an enterprise risk management (ERM) solution, in conjunction with one of the industry-specific methods described above, provides an effective method of institutionalizing a business's risk management process. *Does the business include ERM in its institutionalized methods?*

The first step in this standard requires the practitioner to establish a "context." By using the questions provided in *Operations Due Diligence,* a context of operations risk will be established. *Has the business institutionalized the ISO 31000 risk management standards?*

I felt that *Operations Due Diligence* needed to mention the importance of all of these methods in order to be complete. Whether or not a business favors one of these methods over another or chooses yet some other form is not the subject of this book, and it is left to the readers to research their specific certification requirements. A due diligence assessment is **not** synonymous with a certification assessment for any of the identified formalized methods. Participating in a due diligence assessment does **not** certify the business as a practitioner of these methods. Each of these methods requires the business to attain some level of compliance with the standards of the method in order to claim that it is a certified practitioner. These certifications are an indicator of the maturity of the business, however. Not surprisingly, most of these methods are quality and customer satisfaction oriented. *Does the business follow any formalized methodology such as ISO 9001, CMM/CMMI (ISO/IEC 15504), Six Sigma, TQM, or Lean Manufacturing?*

> A due diligence assessment is **not** synonymous with a certification assessment for any of the identified formalized methods. Participating in a due diligence assessment does **not** certify the business as a practitioner of these methods.

Similarly, certification in one of these methods does not replace the need for a full Operations Due Diligence. Since these methods are targeted to specific practice areas of the business, they are not a certification of all of the infrastructure areas. An internal operations assessment will identify areas of operations risk that might be mitigated by adopting one of these methods.

When compared to a business that has not achieved a similar certification, when a business has been certified in one of these methods, it represents a lower-risk investment because the certification process requires the business to invest in its infrastructure. During an operations assessment, you will need to explore the nature of any compliance and/ or certification claims being made by the business and understand why the business feels these claims are important. Have they made this commitment because it's good business, or were there specific requirements driving them to become certified? Do their customers require a level of process certification? *Is the business certified in the process methodology for the primary market it serves?*

To optimize their operations and improve product quality, all businesses need to institutionalize their processes such that they are followed time and again. Their processes are repeatable. Metrics collected while following repeatable processes should be used to provide a historic baseline that supports the estimation of future expenses and schedule estimates. *Does the business collect process data to support its future cost and schedule estimates?*

It can take years to collect the artifacts required to demonstrate compliance with most of these methods. The certification processes require the business to provide evidence demonstrating a history of implementation on past projects. This becomes a risk if the business needs the certification to qualify for a contract and it doesn't have the artifacts from past projects to demonstrate past performance. A business that claims it is "trying to become CMMI certified" must be able to explain where it is in the certification process. "We have completed two projects, but we need three to qualify." If the business is acquired or changes names as part of an M&A event, you may need to verify that the certification and any qualifying past projects are transferable and that the certification process doesn't have to be started over. *Is the process certification transferable, or will there need to be a new certification assessment conducted after an acquisition?*

Maintaining a certification in one of these methods has significant costs (continuous training and metrics collection, for instance), and you will need to ensure that these costs are reflected in the budget. The effort to institutionalize processes can represent a significant overhead cost for a business, and the return on investment for these efforts can be difficult to measure. It's difficult, for instance, to measure the expense for resolving a software bug that didn't occur in the field because the institutionalized software test process caused the defect to be avoided or the bug was eliminated before the product was shipped (sometimes referred to as the *cost of quality*). Process improvement programs have to be budgeted if they are going to succeed. *Is the cost to maintain the institutionalized processes included in the budget? Does the business monitor product improvement trends, such as reduced defect rates, to justify the ROI for its process improvement program?*

I helped a client business capture and document all of the internal processes from across its entire operation. The business spent time and money to institutionalize its processes in order to qualify for a large government contract it was bidding on. Unfortunately, the business was underbid by a competitor and didn't get the contract. Following the loss, the business never used the documented processes and saw no value in maintaining them. Instead, the business fell back to a mode of ad hoc operations and "just do what has to get done." The business never understood the opportunity it had to improve its operations, which would have made it more competitive. Because it had no baseline processes, it had no baseline data against which to measure the improvement. Welcome to 1903!

Process certification is difficult to justify in a budget negotiation if there is no data to justify the expense. Without an institutionalized process, there are no recurring processes and no means to collect effective metrics. There is a "chicken and egg" problem here. Institutionalizing the operational processes in order to improve efficiency and lower operating expenses makes sense for any business, but providing the rationale to justify the expense often means first getting a management commitment. It requires management vision. Many businesses understand and take the time to institutionalize their processes even if they have no baseline performance data. *How committed is the business to following its institutionalized processes?*

Since it takes time to execute the legacy projects needed for most certifications, it can take years to become a certified method practitioner. This requires a time commitment as well as a budget commitment on the part of the business. The business also has to invest in training its employees, so there must be a strong HR commitment as well. What I look for during an operations assessment is an established process methodology that demonstrates that the business has made an educated decision about the way it will conduct business and is able to produce metrics and other evidence that it is following its institutionalized processes. *If the business is in the certification process, how many legacy projects can it qualify, and how long has it been deploying this methodology?*

In 1987, Congress established the Malcolm Baldrige National Quality Award to promote quality awareness, to recognize quality and business achievements of U.S. businesses, and to publicize the achievements of businesses with successful performance strategies. The Baldrige Award is presented annually to U.S. businesses by the president of the United States. Awards are given in manufacturing, service, small business, education, health care, and nonprofits. *Does the business recognize the connection between managing its processes, quality assurance, customer satisfaction, and improved sales, and has it established goals in these performance areas?*

Process maintenance is typically performed by a process improvement group consisting of members from across the organization. This group uses process feedback to identify improvement areas so that the business is continually challenging itself to perform better. Typically a process improvement group will find more areas needing improvement than there are available resources. By assessing each of the areas needing improvement in terms of the potential risk of not making the improvements, it is possible to prioritize the process improvement plan. Process improvement groups should be populated with representatives from each of the operational groups, which allow the employees responsible for performing a task to define the method they will follow. *Does the business have a process improvement group that meets on a periodic basis? Does the business create an annual process improvement plan?*

The trap that many businesses fall into is that they institutionalize only the product development processes and procedures used by their engineering or manufacturing departments. Remember that the production infrastructure goes beyond engineering and extends across functions such as requirements from sales, marketing, product management, and human resources. The processes that institutionalize the production infrastructure need to span the entire organization and should not be limited solely to the "product side of the house." Similarly, the sales and marketing infrastructure needs to include the processes for preparing bids and proposals, and it should span the full organization from engineering, to manufacturing, to sales, to contracts, and to senior management. If one of these formalized methods is chosen as the sole means of institutionalizing the operations infrastructure, it has to be applied across the entire business. *Is there a list of the existing documented processes, supporting forms or other data, and evidence that the process is being followed across the entire business?*

The value of process management was proven in the munitions factories of World War II. It seems the driving requirement for the manufacture of bombs was that they explode consistently when they were supposed to and not any sooner. This goal was rather important both for the munitions workers who worked on the production lines who didn't want the bombs to explode prematurely and also for the pilots who risked their lives to drop the bombs and wanted them to explode when dropped on the target!

W. Edwards Deming, who had previously worked with Walter Shewhart at Bell Labs, was given the job of defining statistical methods for controlling how bombs were manufactured. By defining standards for the manufacturing process, it was possible to ensure that the production of the bombs was always done in a safe consistent manner.

The quality of the products could then be assured by inspecting the end products, and when problems did occur, they could be resolved by changing the manufacturing process.

This is an extreme example of the ability to improve the manufacturing process by minimizing operations risks by institutionalizing the production infrastructure. A mistake in the process could be deadly. Deming produced evidence that the manufacturing process could be managed to control the quality of the product and mitigate risk.

After World War II, Deming became famous for his work in Japan, helping Japanese manufacturers improve the quality of their automobiles. The early Japanese automobiles manufactures were characterized by their poor quality. By working with the Japanese to apply rigid control over their manufacturing tolerances, Deming was able to improve the quality of the Japanese automobiles such that they eventually outperformed products manufactured with similar specifications but less rigid tolerances in the United States and Europe. *Does the business maintain rigid development standards and defined levels of tolerance for the performance of its products?*

In Chapter 7 I used the Edsel, whose name became synonymous with poor quality, as an example of what happens when a business, even a business the size of Ford, expands beyond the ability of its infrastructure to sustain its operations. Unfortunately, we did not need to look as far back as 1957 to find an example of a business that has outgrown its infrastructure. The same mistake was repeated 50 years later by Toyota.

As a result of Deming's work in Japan during the latter half of the twentieth century, the inexpensive Toyota sedan of the 1960s and 1970s evolved into the Lexus of the twenty-first century.

As its reputation for building high-quality automobiles grew, Toyota began to rapidly expand its manufacturing operations. From 2003 through 2007 Toyota's business expanded rapidly, making it the leading global manufacturer of automobiles. And that's when Toyota's operations infrastructure dramatically failed.

There were numerous reports about the lowered quality of Toyota products but none as dramatic as those resulting from the crash of a 2009 Toyota Lexus. California Highway Patrol Officer Mark Saylor, his wife, daughter, and another family member were driving the Lexus when it rapidly accelerated. The Lexus eventually plummeted over an embankment killing all four occupants. The National Highway Traffic Safety Administration (NHTSA) investigated the crash including a 911 call during which the driver reported he had no brakes, and the NHTSA found that the Toyota had a serious defect causing the crash.

Toyota model names like Lexus, Prius, and Tundra suddenly became the twenty-first-century versions of the Edsel.

This incident was only one of numerous quality and safety issues suddenly being reported by Toyota owners. Toyota model names like Lexus, Prius, and Tundra suddenly became the twenty-first-century versions of the Edsel. The cause of this sudden change in Toyota's image is best explained in the words of its own executives.

In an interview with *Automotive News*, Akia Toyoda, president of Toyota and grandson of its founder, said: "In 2003, we surpassed the 6 million sales mark, and after that the rate of increase kept growing. . . . We look at that as the turning point. . . . When we hit the 6 million mark, we maybe couldn't apply the Toyota Way as thoroughly as we should have."

During his testimony before the Congress in 2010, Toyoda repeatedly attributed Toyota's quality and safety problems to its rapid growth. He said the company could not train enough personnel to keep up with this rapid growth.

From these comments it is clear that Toyota will return to the maintenance of its institutionalized processes and operations infrastructure to mitigate its safety, quality, production, and customer satisfaction risks as the key to sustaining its future operations. *Is the operations infrastructure sufficient to support the business's projected future operations?*

Following a 10-month investigation, the results of further investigation by the NHTSA released in February 2011 stated, "There is no electronic-based cause for unattended high speed acceleration in Toyotas. . . . The problems were mechanical in nature." At the same time, Toyota reported that its profits had dropped "39 percent for the previous quarter."

The damage to Toyota's reputation for building reliable automobiles had a dramatic and costly impact when it failed to predict the risk of outgrowing its operations infrastructure. Toyota's response to the problem was to look inward and to launch improvements to its operations infrastructure including improving the time engineering has to verify new designs, adding new employee training centers, restructuring its management staff to improve accountability, improving its internal problem reporting and communications, establishing cross-functional review teams, and increasing its safety engineering staff.

The actions taken by Toyota in response to its safety issues are in stark contrast to the actions taken by the U.S. automobile manufacturers in response to their economic issues. Toyota, almost instinctively, went to its infrastructure for root cause solutions. The cost of these infrastructure improvements probably seems trivial compared to the loss of public confidence in its vehicles. By contrast, the U.S. manufacturers instinctively looked outward and responded to their problems by launching hybrid and electric vehicle models aimed solely at increasing their market share without making substantial changes to the way they operate their businesses. The automobile manufacturers now seem to have reset the competition along the lines of infrastructure development that the U.S. manufacturers had previously lost.

Summary of the Institutionalized Processes Questions

1. Does the business operate in an ad hoc manner, or does it operate in a determined focused manner that it constantly seeks to improve?
2. Does the business routinely document its operational policies and procedures, and is there evidence that employees are following them?
3. Does the business include ERM in its institutionalized methods?
4. Has the business institutionalized the ISO 31000 risk management standards?
5. Does the business follow any formalized methodology such as ISO 9001, CMM/CMMI (ISO/IEC 15504), Six Sigma, TQM, or Lean Manufacturing?
6. Is the business certified in the process methodology for the primary market it serves?
7. Does the business collect process data to support its future cost and schedule estimates?

8. Is the process certification transferable, or will there need to be a new certification assessment conducted after an acquisition?

9. Is the cost to maintain the institutionalized processes included in the budget?

10. Does the business monitor product improvement trends, such as reduced defect rates, to justify the ROI for its process improvement program?

11. How committed is the business to following its institutionalized processes?

12. If the business is in the certification process, how many legacy projects can it qualify, and how long has it been deploying this methodology?

13. Does the business recognize the connection between managing its processes, quality assurance, customer satisfaction, and improved sales, and has it established goals in these performance areas?

14. Does the business have a process improvement group that meets on a periodic basis?

15. Does the business create an annual process improvement plan?

16. Is there a list of the existing documented processes, supporting forms or other data, and evidence that the process is being followed across the entire business?

17. Does the business maintain rigid development standards and defined levels of tolerance for the performance of its products?

18. Is the operations infrastructure sufficient to support the business's projected future operations?

Review Documents to Be Collected

As part of the due diligence process, the assessment team will request and review a number of operations documents from the business. The following list includes a common set of documents to be requested. This list should be expanded and contracted as required. All effort should be made to identify and review these documents prior to the on-site assessment in order to allow the on-site review to verify that the business complies with its own documentation.

- Organization chart
- Organization mission statements
- Job descriptions
- Current and past customer lists
- Risk management plan and/or process and current data
- All existing documented processes and historic evidence that they have been followed
- Ethics policy
- Performance appraisals for each employee for preceding three years
- A management team skills matrix and a management team skills arachnid
- A list of all of the employee benefits offered by the business

- A list of all full-time, part-time, and contract employees currently employed by the business or employed by the business within the past three years
- The personnel file for all employees
- The performance appraisals for each employee for the preceding three years
- A list of all employees who are currently on performance notices
- A copy of each employee's résumé or CV
- A copy of all employment contracts
- A staffing curve showing staff loading over time and explanations for any downturns in relation to the profitability of the business at the time
- A list by element (salary, bonus, options, and so on) of compensation for each employee for the last three years and a list of all scheduled or promised future compensation
- Pro forma revenue projections for at least the next three years
- A breakdown of the loaded labor rates
- A list of all pending or suspected customer claims based on known product defects
- A copy of all standard document templates, with those identified that have been through a legal review
- A list of the captured intellectual property and copies of all existing patents, copyrights, and trademarks
- A list of all assets the business considers proprietary that have not been captured as intellectual property
- Software development life cycle process descriptions
- Engineering design documents and product artifacts
- Hardware test plans for all products
- Software test plan for all products
- Test bug or deficiency logs
- Customer training plan
- Employee training plan
- Compensation plan
- Sales process
- Marketing plan
- Strategic plan
- Current sales pipeline and lead trend charts

- List of current customers including contact information for key customers
- Profit and loss statement
- Balance sheet
- Pro forma projections
- Cash flow statement
- Capital investment and depreciation schedule
- Policy on financial authority
- Copies of the business's tax returns for the last five years
- All contracts
- All insurance policies
- All present, prior, pending, or potential litigation
- All strategic agreements
- All royalty agreements
- All vendor or reseller agreements
- All nondisclosure agreements
- All employment and labor agreements
- Legal authority policy
- Document retention policy
- Data privacy policy
- Network usage policy

INDEX

ABOUT THE AUTHOR

Jim Grebey is a hands-on executive with a history of success. He has been able to apply his engineering background and analytic skills to become a leading operations analyst and business problem solver with a track record for building high-performance, winning teams. He has accomplished this for both large and small businesses by implementing successful growth strategies, resulting in increased revenues, lowered operating costs, and improved customer satisfaction. As Chapter 1 explains, business operations is a broad field with no single method at its foundation. This is the very essence of the need for this book. Only an executive who has been working "in the trenches," solving operations issues, would be capable of writing this type of book.

Grebey has focused his efforts on improving the sustainability of businesses by improving the infrastructure that guides their continuing operations. He has led online forums, published articles, and presented papers on numerous technical and management subjects.

Grebey was honored to testify before the U.S. Congress as an expert witness following the terrorist attacks of September 11, 2001. His testimony on methods for providing secure identification of transportation workers was given before the Aviation Subcommittee by invitation of Representative John Mica of Florida.

In 2000, Grebey moved to Singapore where he was instrumental in helping manufacturers throughout Asia bring their products to market in the United States, assisting U.S. businesses seeking offshore partners and helping offshore investors find compatible U.S. businesses for investment.

In 2000, Grebey formed Diligent Consulting, which he continues to operate today (now Diligent, Inc.). Through Diligent, he has had the opportunity to work with many businesses, both large and small. His success with Diligent has resulted from his ability and willingness to work hands on with clients to improve their operations.

Grebey has been responsible for presenting clients to investment groups and for supporting their negotiations with investors, and he has participated in numerous M&A due diligence events. Grebey doesn't work as a "touch-and-go" consultant. Instead, he takes an active role in coaching his clients, tugging, pulling, mentoring, and trying to make things happen. The readers of *Operations Due Diligence* will find they get smiles of familiarity on their faces saying, "Yup, been there, done that," and they will relate well to an author who speaks from their shared experiences.